MW00446995

"It's a great art, is rowing. It's the finest art there is. It's a symphony of motion. And when you are rowing well, why it's nearing perfection… And when you reach perfection, you're touching the divine. It touches the you of you. Which is your soul."

— George Pocock (boat designer and builder)

Cover Photo By Charles Came

May you always find calm water

Jen Cuyler

Copyright © 2006 Lew Cuyler
All rights reserved.
ISBN: 1-4196-4425-4

To order additional copies, please contact us.
BookSurge, LLC
www.booksurge.com
1.866.308.6235
orders@booksurge.com

ERNESTINE BAYER

Mother of U.S. Women's Rowing

TABLE OF CONTENTS

Foreword 7

Introduction 14

The Experience of Rowing 17

The Head of the Charles 2001 27

Childhood 30

Philadelphia and Rowing 36

The Philadelphia Girls Rowing Club and its First Race 43

Tina and the Postwar Years 56

A Teddy Bear on Green Lake 63

Ernest Bayer 72

The Road to Vichy 79

Vichy 89

Ernie 99

Tina—Rise and Fall of a Rowing Career 106

Male Chauvinism in the 1970s as Portrayed in *The Oarsman* 115

Move to New Hampshire 121

Arthur Martin 129

AOSA 135

Title IX 144

The University of New Hampshire 147

Gail and Liz 159

Nottingham and The Red Rose Crew 168

The 1976 Olympics 172

Squamscott Scullers and Recognitions 177

Still Competing—Still Winning 184

Carie Graves to the Rescue 189

The Most Unforgettable Row of My Life 192

Ernie Anecdotes 197

Afterword 203

Bibliography and Sources 206

About the Author 208

To Tina, with gratitude and respect.

Ernestine and Tina, 1990　　　　　National Rowing Foundation

AUTHOR'S FOREWORD

The author, Lew Cuyler, takes a break in front of Boathouse Row, Philadelphia, the day
before the Head of the Schuylkill Regatta in October 1997.   Linda Lehman

I HAVE BEEN A SERIOUS ROWER SINCE 1989 WHEN, AT OF FIFTY-
six, I had the opportunity to recapture the feelings for the
sport that I had so loved in school and college. My rowing
experience—I graduated from Amherst in 1955—had ended
long ago. However, in the back of my mind I always wanted to try
it again.

In the meantime, I devoted my life to having a family and
holding down various journalistic jobs as editor, reporter,
or photographer on two daily newspapers and a weekly in
western Massachusetts. In between I was a freelance writer and
photographer. In 1989, upon a promotion to business editor of
The Berkshire Eagle in Pittsfield, my wife and I moved to that
city. I discovered Lake Onota which, end to end, offered two
miles of rowing water. The decision to re-start my rowing career
was a slam dunk.

I wrote a few pieces about rowing, and immediately discovered the frustration of trying to describe the sport to people who assumed I was talking about kayaks or canoes, boats they could understand. Except for Williams College, with its Williamstown campus twenty miles north of the city, which used Lake Onota for its crew program, Pittsfield did not have a rowing culture. Rowing was way outside the city's experience. Therefore, any article I wrote about rowing generated little interest. .

Rowing, to laypersons, is incomprehensible. For starters, rowers face backwards to go forward. Many years ago Frank Howard, then the athletic director at Clemson (South Carolina) University, made the same point when he vociferously opposed a student effort to start a crew.

"Clemson will never support a sport in which people sit on their asses and go backwards," he said, dramatically betraying the level of misunderstanding that still prevails about rowing.

Nevertheless, I kept trying to educate. In 1993, for instance, I wrote an essay entitled "Why Row?"
Here are excerpts:

> 'Athletes Row: All the others play games,' proclaimed a T-shirt at the Thomas Eakins Head of the Schuylkill Regatta Oct. 30, 1993.

> Another reported: 'Row. Life is short.' Dozens of others gave bumper sticker treatment to a sport that defies easy description to non-rowers unaware of the euphoria of sending a boat out from under them in the early morning on a river or lake.

> High level rowing does not come easily. It takes years to achieve the consistent coordination of sliding seat, bladework, and balance required to move a shell through the water gracefully, stroke after stroke. Conversely, it only takes a short time—maybe an hour or two—to know that smooth rowing can happen. It just takes practice...

> ...Why row? The answers are many. Racing is but one

measure and not the motivator for most scullers. For them, and ultimately for me, sculling is unique in the communion of body and mind that takes place in the rapturous environment of water in all of its moods.

The water, the physical effort, and the mental discipline blend to provide a mental high, unlike any other I have ever experienced. Rowing hard in the morning produces chemistry that makes the rest of the day take care of itself.

Most specifically rowing means achieving balance in a skinny, frail boat despite the forces of wind, waves, rain and occasional fog. Rowing means watching the sunrise, slipping through wisps of early dawn mist that hug the water, seeing hills become lush green in the spring and turn to a blaze of color in the autumn. Rowing is the honking of Canada geese, spotting an occasional swan or heron, the stillness of grey November, the anticipation of a summer day.

Rowing is technical; there is so much more to bladework than pulling an oar. That makes women especially good at the sport; they have the patience to learn the technique instead of bulling themselves through the stroke.

Rowing is for life. Ernestine Bayer, 84, 'mother of women's rowing in the U.S.' competed in the three mile Head of the Charles course on Oct. 24...

ERNESTINE BAYER IS MY HEROINE AND MY MUSE.

I met Ernestine Bayer in the early 1990s, at an Alden Ocean Shell regatta in New York state. She exemplified everything I wanted to become in rowing. She was enthusiastic, she was a competitor, she was a good coach, and she was compelled to communicate her feelings about rowing.

In 1995, I retired from the newspaper business, founded a rowing club, continued to compete (mostly in singles), and began selling single shells. I also saw Ernestine from time to time, and concluded that her life had been so important to so many people, both men and women, that someone should get it all down by writing her biography. In 2003, with no one stepping up to the plate, I decided to give myself the assignment.

There followed many interruptions, not the least of which were the responsibilities of keeping both a fledgling rowing business and a fledgling rowing club going. Finally, as 2005 drew to a close, I decided I had to complete the book in 2006.

The work has involved several trips, including one to Vichy, France, in 2003 where I competed in the world masters championships. I have conducted more than fifty interviews; I have read or re-read several books; and I have visited the Bayer household in Stratham, NH several times. I also visited Boathouse Row in Philadelphia, the Mystic (Connecticut) Seaport Museum, and the Princeton, NJ headquarters of US Rowing.

I am grateful for the extraordinary help I have received, and especially thank Tina Bayer for the many conversations we have had about her mother. I also had several interviews with Ernestine before she became ill, the victim of two strokes. As a result, I was unable to re-interview her as the work progressed. Others who have made themselves available for interviews are:

Bernadette Andrews, Debbie Arenberg, Marjorie Pollock Ballheim, Liz Bergen, Daniel J. Boyne, Edward Brainard II, Marjorie Martin Burgard, Mary Colgan, Coleen Fuerst and Jim Dreher, Shep Evans, Herb and Dot Everett, Pat Ferguson, Jack Frailey, Jeanne Friedman, Carie Graves, Mrs. Ephram Hahn Jr., Jeannette Hoover, Gail Ricketson Helfer, Penny and Joe Henwood, Barbara Hoe, Diane Jones, John Kiefer, Pat Koing, Richard Kuhn, Richard LaLonde, Richard Lapchick, Frank Louchheim, Fred Leonard, Vivian Leonard, Micky McGrath, Mike McGill, Charles McIntyre, Darcy McMahon, Holly Metcalf, Bill Miller, Liz Hills O'Leary, Abby Peck, Hart Perry, John Quinn, Joan

Scholl, Joe Sweeney, Sophie Socha Kozak, Peter Van Allen, Bill Stowe, Joanne Wright, and Mary Beth Wethersby.

Four people, especially, were important in the development of this book. My wife, Harriet, an accomplished rower and coach, insisted I create a schedule for myself so that I could no longer put off the task of writing the book. She then patiently lived with the book and my absorption in its writing, production, and promotion; Peter Van Allen, a rower and journalist, and his wife, Jen, of Bryn Mawr, Pennsylvania, who offered me hospitality and insights during my multi-day stay in Philadelphia; and finally, my sister, Juliana McIntyre, who read the almost-finished manuscript and then offered valuable insights into some of its passages and provided observations that were important in reshaping the final manuscript.

US Rowing, through Glenn Merry, its executive director, also generously gave me the use of a desk and a copy machine while I conducted three days of research into its magnificent but uncatalogued collection of old rowing magazines at its Princeton, New Jersey headquarters. Equally generous in giving me space to work was the Mystic Seaport Museum in Mystic, Connecticut, where Hart Perry introduced me to the collection of Ernestine Bayer papers at its G.W. Blunt White Library and other memorabilia that someday will become an exhibit.

I am also indebted to Bill Miller for reading the manuscript and writing an introduction. Bill has lived much of the history that appears in this book.

And finally, profound thanks to Victoria Wright, of Bookmark Services, Housatonic, Massachusetts, this work's chief editor and production manager, for her many words of encouragement during the process of writing and her expertise in shepherding it through the publishing process, and to Robin O'Herin, Robin

O'Herin Designs, Lee, Massachusetts; Nicole O'Neil, Dolce Media, Pittsfield, Massachusetts; and Dianne Harris, DeSigner Graphics, Hinsdale, Massachusetts whose talents has added visual life to the book. My thanks also go to Hugh Henry, account representative for BookSurge Publishing, an Amazon.com company, who turned all of our efforts into a book.

I have attempted accuracy in my reporting of Ernestine's life. Inevitably errors creep in despite extensive fact-checking. Any errors are inadvertent. I take full responsibility for any conclusions I have expressed in the following pages.

LEW CUYLER
Pittsfield, Massachusetts
June 2006

P.S. Michelle Price, a rowing acquaintance, is an artist who lives and works in Vermont. A single sculler, her daily rows inspire her paintings, drawings and installations. She has this to say about rowing and art:

> "My artwork is about the exploration of opposing forces,
> a dichotomy of energies coming together to create balance
> and harmony. Push, pull, male, female, strong, weak,
> the endless array of rivaling influences that exist in
> our universe. My paintings emerge with dark shapes
> against light shapes, texture over smooth surfaces, and
> complementary color schemes that define positive and
> negative space. Chaotic marks mingle with quiet sections
> and transparent paint hovers over opaque planes. The
> subject matter for these conflicts is the art of rowing. I
> investigate the forms of the boats, their hard, sleek, stiff
> surfaces, against the soft fluid ever changing water. The
> combination of shapes fascinates me. The lightweight
> rowing craft is propelled through the heavy water with the
> look of grace and effortlessness even though amazing force
> is exerted to make the motion happen. Rowers seek to mesh

disagreeing serves to create impeccable balance, speed and run. It is a very difficult and technical endeavor. It is truly akin to painting. You can see where you have been but don't know where you are going. You are pushing really hard, then pulling back gently. You hold tight but then soften your grip. It takes obsessive practice to master the skill and you must be totally present in the moment to allow the variety of forces to entangle with each other for the desired outcome. Then you will achieve flow.

Thus, through my rowing images I experience the great art of painting, a fine art. There is a symphony of motions and strokes. When I am painting well, it is nearing perfection. When I reach that perfection I am touching the divine, and it touches that in me, which is my soul."

Boathouse Row, Philadelphia   City of Philadelphia

INTRODUCTION

by Bill Miller

I BECAME ACQUAINTED WITH ERNEST, ERNIE, AND TINA BAYER IN **1969,** when we traveled to Austria for the European Championships, my first international rowing excursion. It didn't take long for me to realize that this was rowing's First Family. Ernestine Bayer, Mother of US Women's Rowing very nicely and accurately describes the many reasons why.

For the 2000-2001 edition of the American Rower's Almanac, I was asked to write a piece about the twentieth century's ten most notable people. Wow! Just ten. With a sharp pencil I got the list down to thirty. Now, to get to ten. So I listed top "notable" people first. There are three whom I could easily select for the list in the Top Ten. I started with George Pocock, boat-builder, coach, and mentor—loved by all who rowed in North America. Next, John B. Kelly, Sr. (I limited the precious spots to one family member so Kelly Jr. wasn't included). JBK, Sr. defined the American rowing "can do" spirit (two 1920 Olympic Gold Medals in an hour). Third on my list was easy: Ernestine Bayer, Mother of Women's Rowing in the US.

Soon after the Almanac's publication, I received a call from Ernestine and Tina thanking me for the very nice comments that I wrote. With all modesty, Ernie exclaimed that she did not deserve such high acclaim, but as you will read, she certainly does. In my conversation with her, I asked whether she would like to travel from her home in Stratham, New Hampshire to Raymond, Maine to spend the day as a guest at my rowing camp. It's an instructional program for high school-aged kids. She said she'd be honored.

At noon, I announced to the campers that we had special guests, Ernestine and Tina Bayer, who would speak in the recreation hall. About seventy youngsters sat on benches and were dead quiet as Ernestine and Tina mesmerized them with stories about their experiences. Even the coaches and counselors sat quietly hanging on to every word. After it was over some of the girls went up to greet them and to ask for their autographs. One girl came up to me and thanked me for arranging the experience. She said Ernestine was her idol. She had written a high school research paper about Ernestine and to meet her in person was one of her greatest thrills. I'm not sure who was more thankful for the event, the campers and coaches or Ernestine and Tina. It was a very special moment.

A few months later I called the Bayer household to chat and Tina answered. "Bill, Mom and I were just talking about you!" exclaimed Tina. "We're cleaning out the attic and we have a bunch of our rowing memorabilia that we'd like to donate to the National Rowing Foundation. Can you drive up to Stratham?"

"Sure," was my answer. We spent the better part of a day rummaging through boxes of newspaper clippings, photographs, medals, official's badges, and more. With each object, a delightful story followed. It was a joy to reminisce and learn about all Ernestine's experiences.

When I received a call from Lew Cuyler describing his intentions to write the story of Ernestine's life, I was elated. It was time for someone to chronicle her fabulous achievements. Lew has collected many great bits of information about the Bayers and has captured their personalities, and those of others, perfectly. You'll enjoy reading about Ernestine Bayer, one of the most delightful and memorable people I ever met.

ABOUT BILL MILLER...

Bill Miller of Duxbury, Massachusetts has been associated with rowing for the past forty-one years. He began rowing in 1965 at Northeastern University, was crew captain in 1969, and then a member of the national team from 1969 through 1975. He has coached at MIT and Boston University, and in 1982, coached the national lightweight eight. He managed the US National Men's Team for two years, at championships in Amsterdam and in Bled, Yugoslavia.

In 1989, he founded the Northeast Rowing Center on Crescent Lake in Raymond, Maine. In 1992, he co-founded the Friends of Rowing History. He is cofounder and coach of the Duxbury Bay Rowing program. Since 2000, he has been a member of the National Rowing Foundation board.

Singles race on the Charles, 2005   Lew Cuyler

THE EXPERIENCE OF ROWING

Lake Onota, Pittsfield, MA   Lew Cuyler

ROWING, LIKE FALLING IN LOVE, DEFIES A PRECISE DEFINITION. People know when they fall in love but they are unable to explain exactly why they feel that way or how it all happened. They only know that it is so. The rowing stroke has those same elements. Coaches can tell rowers all about the stroke, how to grasp the oar, how to let it fall into the water, how to release it from the water, and how to prepare for the next stroke. They can lead rowers to the threshold but they cannot cross that threshold for them. The rower has to discover the threshold and then cross over.

Many rowers use the word "connect" to describe what they do. Mind, body, shell, oar, and water all connect in the perfect stroke. When it happens, the rower and the shell feel weightless as the motion takes over. The rower goes into a zone, instinctively trying to hang on to that feeling, stroke after stroke. The work of rowing is hard, but it can feel effortless because of the help received from the momentum of the shell, the push of the legs, the swing of the body.

Rowers sit on a "slide," a little seat that goes back and forth on tracks during the stroke. This enables them to use their legs for power, as opposed to their backs or arms, which would bear the brunt of the work if they were on a fixed seat. The slide was invented in 1870 by John C. Babcock of the New York Athletic Club. Before it came into use, some rowers would grease the seat of their pants to achieve more work from their legs.

The modern rowing stroke is very efficient, allowing each part of the body to do what it does best. The legs are the strongest part of the body, followed by the back and then the arms. The legs provide each stroke with its initial momentum as they push against the foot-stretcher creating the leverage that pushes the shell forward. At the beginning of each stroke the upper body is relaxed. The oar blade "falls into" the water and as soon as it is seated, legs apply pressure to the oar shaft, which is contained, but not gripped, in the rower's hand or hands (depending upon whether there is one oar or two). The legs initiate the drive and then, at a precise moment, the rower's back swings towards the bow of the shell pivoting from the hips, supplementing the leg-initiated pressure on the oar. Finally, in the last part of the stroke, the rower's arms pull it all together, bringing the oar grip to the lower part of the rower's rib cage, then pushing the grip down to release the oar from the water. The rower then feathers the oar (turning it parallel to the surface of the water), and pushes hands forward to prepare for the recovery, or the trip back up the slide to initiate the next stroke.

Slide control on the recovery is essential for good rowing. If the slide moves too fast towards the stern of the shell, which means moving in the opposite direction the shell is traveling, there will be "check" because the weight moving too fast towards the stern is counter to the shell's forward progress. The recovery, therefore, must be gentle and in tune with the shell's speed through the water.

If done correctly, the shell moves forward at the same speed the rower or rowers move backward, creating the sensation of being light, of being totally in tune with the elements of body, boat, water, speed. Being in tune produces an exhilaration of spirit, a sense of triumph and well-being which lasts for hours after the experience.

People really can't explain why, but many of them become "hooked" or obsessed by rowing. They want to do it again and again. This is what happened to Ernestine Bayer. This is what she wanted to happen to everyone else she met during her long life.

... AND RACING

Humans have always wanted to race, whether on foot, in a boat, in a car, on skis, or in the air. Racing has always been a measure of ability. The place at the finish line doesn't lie. Neither does the clock.

And so it is with rowing. Team rowers, men and women, are generally tall people with large muscles whose bodies provide maximum leverage and strength to the oars. They must also subvert their individuality to make a boat go fast. In contrast, coxswains are small. They need to be smart, with the ability to make quick decisions under pressure. Above all they must have an "attitude." The coxswain seat is no place for people who are shy.

In the crew shells, the coxswains have tremendously important roles to play. They must have the skills to steer straight courses, a piece of work that is more easily said than done because of current, wind, traffic, and, possibly, the uneven stroking of the crew. They must keep track of the race, telling the crew where they are. They must push the crew, inspiring the rowers in whatever way they can. As they overtake a boat they might yell "we have them by a seat, give me another." If the race is close on the course, they must make split decisions about undertaking risky maneuvers that, if successful, mean they will overtake a competitor or go through a bridge arch first.

The second important person in a team shell is the stroke, the rower closest to the stern. Strokes strive for great technique and great rhythm. They need both because every rower in the shell can see the stroke oar and must follow it precisely if they are to attain maximum speed.

There are three main parts to most rowing races: the start, the settle, and the finish. Typically they are rowed on 1,000 and 2,000 meter courses, translating into slightly less than one mile and slightly more. Longer races of two to three miles, called "head races," are popular events in the fall. In addition, there are many rowers who enjoy open water and ocean races in wider and shorter rowing shells that can cope with rough water conditions.

In the shorter races with three to six shells, the boats start from a dead stop. Either their sterns are held by someone on floats at the start or they are started from the shore after a judge lines them up.

The starts involve a series of short strokes to achieve momentum as quickly as possible followed by a series of power strokes to gain an advantage. A typical start might mean, half, half, three-quarters, three-quarters, full, referring to the sequence of strokes needed for maximum momentum with the full stroke reached at the fifth count. A sprint with a high stroke count—perhaps twenty-eight or thirty strokes per minute in a single, or thirty-eight to forty-two in an eight—follows as rowers in each shell strive for an early lead.

By this time, hearts are beating rapidly and rowers are beginning to make the transition between anaerobic and aerobic breathing, a condition formerly known as first wind and second wind. In any event, rowers are breathing hard by the end of the start sequence and it is time to "settle," the term for the transition between higher and lower stroke rates.

In shells without a coxswain, the rowers are only slightly aware of where they are. They can see the shells behind them; they can use their peripheral vision to see the shells beside them; but they cannot see any shell ahead of them. Buoyed courses help because then rowers can steer by looking straight backwards at the buoys. Turning their heads to see is only done if absolutely necessary because head turns interfere with the motion of the boat and interrupt the rhythm of the stroke. Some scullers use rearview mirrors attached to their hats; some find them helpful, others do not.

During the body of the race there may be two or three power drives to overtake a leader or beat someone to a bridge. Finally, with perhaps a hundred meters to go, rowers start their final drives, powering their shell through to the finish. When they cross the finish line they should have nothing left. They come to a stop, they row no more strokes, some collapse over their oars. All rest for at least a minute before paddling away.

Ernestine Bayer loved to race. Jeanne Friedman, now rowing coach at Mt. Holyoke College in Massachusetts, recalled that in 1996, when Ernie was eighty-seven years old, she was rowing with her in a double during the "Row as One" camp for women at Mt. Holyoke.

"I thought we were just going out for a paddle," said Friedman. "Then an eight goes by and Ernie yells out, 'How about a race? We challenge you.' And right away we go to it. Holly Metcalf, the director of the program, gave me a stern look of disapproval when we arrived at the dock after the row because she had told me just to take her out 'for a paddle'. All I could say was, 'I didn't do it. She did.'"

ROWING VOCABULARY AND PRIMER

Non-rowers who dive into the text of this book should arm themselves with a rowing vocabulary. Like all nautical subjects, rowing speaks its own language. Therefore, to make things easier, I offer a primer that will start with a glossary or commonly used terms.

BOW: The forward section of the shell and the first part to cross the finish line. Most rowing shells have "bow balls" to prevent injury should someone be struck by the sharp bow end of the shell.

BUTTON: A wide collar on the oar that keeps it from slipping through the oarlocks.

CATCH: The beginning of the stroke, when the oar "catches" the water.

CRAB: The name given when a rower's oar becomes stuck in the water just before its extraction at the end of the stroke. It usually happens when the rower begins to turn the oar before extracting the blade from the water. The surface water then combines with the momentum of the shell to push the oar down as if a crab had grabbed its blade. When a shell is traveling fast, the crab can almost stop the motion as if brakes were suddenly applied. Even worse it can create leverage on the shaft that can lift the rower out of the shell and dump him or her unceremoniously into the water.

DOUBLE: Shell designed for two rowers, each with two oars. Full name is double sculls.

DECK: The part of the shell a t the bow and stern that is covered with fiberglass cloth or a thin plastic.

COXSWAIN: Usually a smaller person whose job is to sit in the stern section of the shell or lie in the bow section and steer the shell. Coxswains also keep track of position during races and generally direct the race plan including when to call for power strokes. Small people with 'attitude" make the best candidates.

EIGHTS: The glory shells containing eight sweep rowers and a coxswain. These are the fastest shells on the water.

FEATHER: When the oar blade is in its non-stroking flat position above the surface of the water during the recovery from the stroke while the rower prepares for the next sequence.

FOURS: Four oared shells, two on the port side, two on the starboard. Most fours have coxswains, who either sit in the rear section of the shell or are semi-prone in the forward section.

METRIC: The distance of rowing courses is measured in meters, not feet. One meter is 39.37 inches. 1,000 meters is .621 miles. 2,000 meters is 1.242 miles.

OARS: Used to drive the shell forward. Rowers do not use paddles. Modern oar blades are mostly hatchet shaped. The oar plants itself in the water, the oarlock is the fulcrum, and the oar shaft becomes the lever to push the shell forward.

OARLOCKS: Contain and keep the oar in place.

OARLOCK GATE: The small bar across the top of the oarlock that keeps the oar from popping out.

PAIR: Shell designed for two sweep rowers, one port, one starboard. Occasionally you will see a "pair with" meaning there will be a seat for a coxswain in the stern section of the shell.

PORT: The left side of the shell if looking towards the bow.

QUAD: A four with scullers, meaning that it is driven by eight oars. The bow rower steers and generally directs the effort of the crew.

QUAD WITH: A quad with a coxswain.

RIGGERS: As in outriggers. These protrude from the sides of the shell to give the oar shafts their maximum leverage. There are "wing" riggers that are single units that go across the two gunwales of the shells and triangular shaped riggers that are bolted on to each side of the shell.

RUN: Run is the distance the shell moves during one stroke. You can identify a run by the distance between the puddles made by the same oar. Rowers seek to achieve a maximum run by using smooth, as opposed to choppy, strokes.

SCULLS: The oars single scullers use.

SCULLER: Name given to rowers who use two oars.

SHELL: All sliding seat boats are called shells. However, as on a beach there are many different kinds of shells.

SEATS: In the team boats, seats are counted down from the bow which is No. 1 seat.

SINGLE: Shell designed for single rower only.

SKEG: Also called fin. The small keel in the stern section of most rowing shells that keeps the shell on track. Without the skeg or fin, the shell can "wig-wag" in the water with each stroke.

SQUARE: When the oar blade is perpendicular to the water, about to make a stroke, or its position when in the water during the stroke.

STARBOARD: The right side of the shell if looking towards the bow.

STERN: The rear of the boat. The direction the rowers face.

STRAIGHT FOUR: A four without a coxswain. In that case the bow rower steers with his or her foot-plate that has cables that run through pulleys and then attach to the rudder.

STRETCHER OR FOOT-STRETCHER: Where the rower's feet go. The stretcher consists of two inclined footrests which hold the rower's shoes. The shoes are bolted on to the footrests.

STROKE: The rower closest to the coxswain or to the stern

in non-coxed shells is called the stroke. Strokes have the responsibility of establishing the pace by determining the strokes per minute. All of the other rowers can see the stroke oar and be so guided.

STROKE RATE: This refers to the number of strokes per minute. Twenty strokes per minute is slow; forty strokes is fast. The body of most races is between twenty-six and thirty-two for singles, twenty-eight and thirty-eight for the team shells.

SWEEP: Name given to rowers who use only one oar. In this case there must be at least two rowers in the shell, one for each side of the boat.

SWEEP OARS: Oars used by sweep rowers.

SWING: The elusive, hard-to-define feeling when near-perfect synchronization of motion occurs in the shell, enhancing performance and speed. The rower feels almost weightless. Once they feel the swing, rowers spend many hours trying to re-capture the experience.

WHERRY: A smaller, wider, heavier, single rowing shell, with pointed bow and stern. Regarded as a single scull for novices.

CHAPTER 1:
THE HEAD OF
THE CHARLES 2001

Ernestine Bayer finishes first in her age group at Head of Charles, Oct. 1992. She was 83.
Bayer Family Files

DID YOU HEAR THAT?" THE TALL BLONDE WITH A PONYTAIL exclaimed. "That's so cool!" "What's that you say, girl?" her companion, equally tall but a brunette, responded. Both wore loose-fitting sweatshirts indicating to all that they were rowers for the University of Connecticut women's eight. Both were so consumed by the excitement of the day that they could not be still, not even for a minute.

This was their first Head of the Charles regatta, the Cambridge, Massachusetts event that is the largest rowing classic in the world. They had arrived two hours earlier and had just finished unloading and rigging the eight-oared shell they would race the next day, October 22, 2001. On their way to the vendor tents, they had paused to buy sandwiches and drinks, and were now watching the doubles races while scarfing down lunch. On Magazine Beach that sunny fall afternoon, the club races seemed but a footnote to the colorful carnival of shells, trailers, rowers, tents, vendors, rubberneckers, and reunions everywhere. For these two women rowers, in the full flush of their youth, watching the doubles was just one moment among many of the rowing world's most exciting weekend.

Oblivious to anyone listening, their conversation resumed.

"Hear that clapping and shouting down there?" said the first girl. "The announcer just said that the double is being stroked by a ninety-two year old woman. Can you imagine?"

"Ninety-two years old! No way," said the brunette, laughing off the impossibility.

The double was approaching their vantage point. The clapping and shouting swelled.

"Go, Ernie," the crowd yelled.

And indeed, there she was, white-haired Ernestine Bayer, stroking the double with her partner, Abby Peck, the Wellesley women's crew coach and former Olympian. Their near-flawless rowing seemed almost effortless.

"Yay, Ernie Bayer, go for it!" the older guy behind them yelled. "You're looking good. Pow-wer, pow-wer!"

The blonde turned to the older guy.

"Who's Ernie Bayer?" she asked.

"She's the mother of women's rowing in this country," the older guy replied. "She's the one who made it possible for you to row. She founded the first women's rowing club in America. Now women are about half the competitive rowing population in the US, and Ernie had a lot to do with that. ... Go Ernie!"

he shouted, adding an exclamation point to his quick rowing history lesson.

"Awesome," said the brunette. "Do you know her?"

"A little," he said. "I met her in 1992 at a regatta in New York State. I found myself standing next to her watching women's singles races. She commented on the stroke of each woman, picking out what they were doing right and what they were doing wrong. I was impressed with her knowledge.

"When she started rowing, everyone said, 'Women can't row,'" he mused. "She made liars out of all of them."

"I coach high school women rowers," he continued. "They live in the Now, but I make sure they know the history of their sport. I tell them all about Ernestine Bayer. She's an icon."

"Good luck in your race tomorrow," he concluded. "Row it for Ernestine. She's the one who made it happen, and now you have seen her."

"Go, Ernie!" they shouted before they moved on.

"Hey, thanks for telling us about her," said the blonde.

Abby Peck later said that the race was a rare experience. "The wave of applause was so fitting. I felt honored to be in the shell with her, enabling her to hear the salute she so richly deserved. I saw several photos of us rowing that race. In each one, Ernie is obviously pulling like mad. And she's grinning."

CHAPTER 2:
<u>CHILDHOOD</u>

*Ernie was four when this photo was taken. Her
brother Gus is astride the pony.*
Bayer Family Files

E RNESTINE STEPPACHER WAS BORN IN PHILADELPHIA ON
March 25, 1909, a seven pound baby, the second
child of Henry Steppacher, a paper salesman,
and his wife, Rosetta. Her first home was on
Hollywood Street, a tree-lined side street of row houses on the
outskirts of the neighborhood known as Strawberry Mansion,
near Fairmount Park.

The world had just embarked upon the twentieth century,
which would see the development of flight, worldwide
communications, television, fast food restaurants, and rowing
shells made of high tech materials. Most homes did not yet
have electricity or telephones. Few families had cars. Ominous

rumblings in Europe were still barely audible in the United States. Within months of Ernie's fifth birthday World War I would erupt, and the old order would begin to disintegrate.

But at the dawn of the century, the role of men was unchallenged. They ran the businesses, made the inventions, fought, governed, and became athletic heroes. They were also the authority figures in virtually every family. Women were the helpmeets and the civilizing influences, responsible for the household, for manners, and for the day-to-day upbringing of children.

Rosetta steppacher, who was already thirty-eight when ernie WAS born, was a woman of her time. She was mother to a son and a daughter. Her views on the future of her children were mirrors of her society's norms. Her son would be a man of affairs and her daughter, Ernestine, would be a woman in charge of her household but not of her husband. She never encouraged Ernestine to do anything athletic.

Her daughter, however, turned out to be a puzzle. She wouldn't wear pinafores like other little girls. She disdained sewing and similar feminine skills. It was obvious that with her high cheekbones, black hair, and luminous dark eyes she would be a beauty, but she did not act like one. Instead of doing girlish things, she much preferred to join the neighborhood boys in a game of ball. They tolerated her not because they liked her, but because she was so persistent. She made it impossible for them to say no. Little did they know that legions of males from all walks of life in succeeding years would also find it impossible to say no to a woman who had refused to take no for an answer almost from the minute she was born.

Ernie Bayer turned ninety-seven on March 25, 2006. Her memories of a life of rowing are vivid. But she also remembers being four years old and watching her brother Gus, eighteen months her senior, sitting astride a pony for his photo to be taken. The entrepreneurial photographer owned the pony and used it as a prop, thus separating himself from others in his profession. Ernie remembers the photo not for the childhood scene of her brother, but for how angry she became when her mother would not allow her to be photographed in a similar pose. Her mother was adamant. No, she told her daughter, such a pose is not ladylike. That was to be the first of many childhood episodes when her mother admonished her to be more ladylike and Ernie stoutly refused.

She also remembers that when she was little she very much wanted a bicycle just like her brother's, but her mother again refused, on the grounds that riding a bicycle was not "ladylike." Nevertheless, she decided without permission to take her brother's bicycle—a racing bike with no brakes—for a ride. Her brother's friends tattled on her, and she recalls her mother's harsh scolding. At her teacher's insistence she did stop rollerskating to school—not because it was unladylike, but because her skates made too much noise under her desk.

The family moved from quiet, residential Hollywood Street to West Lehigh Avenue, a wide commercial boulevard not far away. Her parents opened a card and gift shop on the ground floor of the building. The route that Ernie walked to and from school featured bakeries, German confectioners, and ice cream parlors, and she would regularly stop on her way home and have an ice cream soda. On summer evenings, she would accompany her father to see the Phillies play at Connie Mack Stadium a few blocks away.

Gus, her brother, had an easier childhood, despite frequent illness in his early years. Rosetta Steppacher made sure he had every privilege she could muster including, much to Ernie's dismay, fresh peas; Ernie was served canned peas. Gus grew to be a talented runner, winning an athletic scholarship to Holy Cross College in Worcester, Massachusetts, where his record for the mile stood for many years. He went on to become a self-made man and a millionaire. He died at the age of seventy-seven from a malignant brain tumor.

In contrast, Ernie dropped out of high school at the age of fifteen—keeping her failure to complete her education a secret for most of her life—and went to work at a bank as a "runner." She would take a message for another bank and literally run through downtown Philadelphia to deliver it, await a response, and run back. She won a promotion to the stocks and bonds department, where she clipped bond coupons for the owners and attached them to the paperwork. The job was reserved for employees whom the bank considered responsible, because the coupons were negotiable. She also attended a secretarial school and became a top-notch secretary.

She lived at home and when her family went to the New Jersey shore for its summer vacation, she commuted daily by train to Philadelphia. She loved to dance, to run in track meets, and to swim. One day at the Jersey shore she swam so far out that she did not hear the lifeguards' warning whistle and they had to come out in the lifeboat and herd her closer to shore where they could keep watch.

Eventually, overcoming a number of male-inspired obstacles, she adopted rowing as her sport, enjoying the rapture of the freedom of movement made possible by water and a sliding seat rowing shell. Almost from the first stroke, rowing became first an obsession and then a calling as she recognized the potential it held for empowering women to achieve. Her daughter, Tina, believes the obsession with rowing was a rebellion against her childhood. Ernie did not want to grow up as the "lady" her mother wanted her to become.

There's a bittersweet ending to the story. Ernestine, in the view of her mother, continued her "unladylike" ways marching to new frontiers when she became not only a good rower, but a pioneer in the sport for women. Her activities, because they were so unusual at the time, were chronicled in numerous newspaper stories. Her mother never commented on the stories, despite having long since given up her notion of creating a ladylike daughter.

When Rosetta died, Ernie had to sort through her belongings. Among them was an envelope filled with yellowed clippings. On its face was a scrawl in her mother's handwriting.

"For Ernie, when I am dead," she had written, a testimony to a mother's pride in her unladylike and rebellious daughter.

Unladylike and rebellious she may have been by the standards that prevailed in her mother's society, but she was to emerge as a woman of the twentieth century, standing tall for womanhood and knowing what she was about. There are countless women out there now, young and old, standing equally tall, but in Ernie's day as a young woman, both her refusal to accept male version of a woman's place and her determination were rare.

Physically, Ernie is arresting. At five feet, five inches, she is somewhat small in stature, weighing about 130 pounds. Today, when most competitive women rowers are taller and heavier, her adult size would not indicate rowing potential. However, she grew fast as a girl and at an early age was nicknamed "the big baked bean."

As an adult, her looks attracted notice. When she was young, her hair was black; by age sixty, it had turned white. Dark brown flashing eyes that light up the space she occupies combine with a spontaneous devil-may-care smile for an arresting presence that is the hallmark of her life.

She carried the women's banner for rowing by sheer force of her vivacious personality. To meet Ernie is to be engaged immediately, to be captivated by the enthusiastic rush reflected in her every movement. Part of her style is merriment. She tells stories with gusto; she laughs at herself and her own shortcomings. She is perceptive and direct. What she says, she means. She is totally honest.

She tells the story, for instance, of persuading the Head of the Charles committee in Boston to allow the Aldens—distinctly a non-racing species of shell—to race early in the morning before the grand event.

The Charles race attracts the best scullers in the world who row the best shells in the world. There simply is no spot in the program for the casual rowers, who row primarily for enjoyment and accordingly, prefer the slow speed and the security of the Alden recreational shell. Although in its way, the Alden Ocean Shell is as important to the sport of rowing, the Alden culture is not the Head of the Charles culture.

The committee never officially accepted the Aldens into the race. Ernie pointed out that the Aldens could be in their own race at seven in the morning, with the start an hour before the big race, and then it could be an Alden race. With this arrangement, she said, the two rowing cultures would not intrude upon each other.

The committee then approved. Since 1972, the Alden race has gone off without incident at seven, with eighty rowers finishing the three-mile course well before the start of the main event and, in the process, giving the Alden rowers a taste of the big banana that is the Head of the Charles.

Was she surprised by the Head of the Charles decision? Yes, she was, she says, then adds with a chuckle of enjoyment, "They must have been nuts ... but don't you ever print that!"

CHAPTER 3:
PHILADELPHIA AND ROWING

Oarswomen from the Philadelphia Girls Rowing Club row an eight past the venerable male-oriented Boathouse Row on Philadelphia's Schuylkill River in 1966.

Bayer Family files

I N THE 1930S, IT WAS UNTHINKABLE FOR A WOMAN, ESPECIALLY a bank office clerk whose place was to help businessmen make things happen, to challenge a culture so deeply entrenched as the one that prevailed on Boathouse Row, Philadelphia.

But that is exactly what Ernestine Bayer did.

For nearly a century, Philadelphia's Boathouse Row had existed as the proud cradle of rowing in America, embracing a male-only culture that had first flourished in Greece in the early days of rowing and then in England before the sport moved to the United States.

Those early Philadelphia rowers were the products of rowing history that dates back to Greek and Roman times when the mighty warships, called triremes, were powered principally by rowers stroking to the beat of a drum. Occasionally, their efforts were augmented by sail when the wind was right. The triremes had battering rams on their bows, and the idea was for three banks of rowers to propel the ships as fast as they could in an effort to ram the smaller crafts of their opponents. Contrary to popular belief most of those early rowers were members of the upper middle class and not the slaves and prisoners so often depicted. Even so, there were some who were conscripted and still others who were prisoners. Whatever their class, they were the power for the warships.

More modern rowing started on the Thames River in London in the early nineteenth century when the bargemen, who ferried goods and people across the Thames during the week, began racing for sport on Sundays, frequently wagering to make their efforts worthwhile. The sport was adopted by the great universities of Oxford and Cambridge and then exported to the United States, where Harvard and Yale engaged in the first intercollegiate competition, a rowing race on Lake Winnepesaukee in New Hampshire in 1852.

The Schuylkill (properly pronounced *school-kill*, but more commonly, *skoo-kl*) River became a viable body of water for rowing in 1822. Just downstream from what would become Boathouse Row, the city constructed a dam to protect the waterworks built in 1805 following a devastating yellow fever epidemic in 1793. As part of the waterworks development, Philadelphia also bought land along the riverbank, and then continued to expand its holdings by acquiring estates overlooking the river, developing the tract that is now Fairmount Park.

The result of the dam was four miles of a superb rowing environment offering protection from wind, as well as long, straight stretches for racing. Only a few years after completion of the waterworks project, the Schuylkill began to attract rowers who had known the sport in Europe. Their gathering place was a riverside tavern called the Rialto House on the east bank, situated in a neighborhood then known as Faire Mounte. Gradually, the rowers began to form clubs. Fairmount was organized in 1870; Pennsylvania Barge Club, was founded in 1861; Crescent, 1867; Bachelors Barge Club, 1853; University Barge Club, 1854; Malta Boat Club, 1863; Vesper Boat Club, 1865; College Boat Club, 1872; Undine Barge Club, 1856; The Sedgley Club, 1867; and Penn AC, originally the West Philadelphia Barge Club, 1871.

Joe Sweeney, a Boathouse Row historian, wrote that "the first organized boat races in the U.S. took place in New York in the mid 1700s by professional bargemen. Amateur boat clubs were formed in Boston, New York, and Philadelphia in the 1830s. University of Pennsylvania (then known as The College, Academy and Educational Trust) rowing history dates back to 1760, when a challenge was issued to New York for a six mile race. The first organized regatta, sponsored by the Amateur Boat Club, was held on the Schuylkill River on November 12, 1835, in which the Blue Devil club rowed its boat of that name, and seven eight-oared barges took part. Another race took place between Devil and Imp Barge clubs in 1839. The same year, two fours with coxswains rowed from New York to race on the Schuylkill. Some sources indicate that earlier contests had taken place between the University of Pennsylvania and the Atlanta Boat Club of New York City. Rowing started at Yale and Harvard in 1843 and 1844 respectively. They raced each other in 1852."

The Schuylkill Navy, an association of rowers who belonged to nine clubs, was started in 1858 with the objective of securing united action among the clubs. The Navy incorporated in 1882 as the first amateur athletic organization in the United States. Other highlights were 1859, the date of the first Schuylkill

Navy regatta; 1873, the first national regatta; 1876, the first international race. The National Association of Amateur Oarsmen, the first governing body for the sport, was formed in 1873 in Philadelphia, in part because the increasing popularity of professional rowing created the need for rules of navigation, the management of races, and working agreements among the clubs.

Rowing in the U.S. reached a new height in the late nineteenth century with the development of the sliding seat in 1870, the innovation of John C. Babcock of the New York Athletic Club. The sliding seat enabled rowers to use their legs for the principal power behind the stroke. The result was they could make the shells go faster and the faster speeds demanded more skills from the rowers. In the late nineteenth century, professional rowing became popular with regattas that attracted thousands of enthusiastic spectators for the events in Boston, New York, and Philadelphia. The races commanded huge headlines in the daily press. Wagering was the draw and thousands of dollars were won and lost. Abruptly, however, the professional sport declined, the result of scandals associated with fixing races or destroying the shells of the favorites. The decline had an unintended benefit: hundreds of the former professionals became collegiate coaches and, as a result, intercollegiate rowing for men grew in popularity.

Thomas Eakins, one of America's best known nineteenth century painters, who lived in his native Philadelphia, contributed substantially to the sport's popularity with a series of powerful paintings between 1870 and 1874. These depicted rowers in various kinds of shells on the Schuylkill, some of them well-known professionals.

Dominating the twentieth century rowing history in Philadelphia were two larger-than-life greats, John B. Kelly senior and junior, who, by virtue of their rowing accomplishments, had tremendous influence. A statue of Kelly senior in a single scull occupies a prominent place overlooking the Schuylkill race course near the Columbia Bridge. In the 1920 Olympics, he became the only man ever to win both singles and doubles events, taking home two gold medals. He then went on to repeat the doubles victory in the 1924 games, taking home a third. He also fathered a famous family, including his son John Junior, also an Olympic medalist and a powerhouse on Boathouse Row, and his daughter, the late Grace Kelly, the movie actress who married Prince Rainier of Monaco and became Princess Grace.

The junior Kelly, born in 1927, began rowing in his youth and went on to win a number of rowing medals, taking the US national singles sculls title eight times: in 1946, 1948, 1950, and 1952–1956. In the 1956 Olympics in Melbourne, Australia, he won a bronze medal in single sculls; he also won gold medals twice in single sculling in the Pan American games. Two of his notable accomplishments were single scull wins in 1947 and 1949 at the Henley Regatta in England, thus avenging his father, who had been barred from the Henley in 1920 on grounds that he was a "bricklayer" and thus considered "NOCD," the acronym standing for "Not Our Class, Dear." At the time, the senior Kelly was the owner of a construction company, a fact ignored by the Henley organizers.

Today's boathouses, most of them built in the latter part of the nineteenth century in the Victorian Gothic style required by the city's Park Commission, replaced the original wooden boatsheds which, by the 1860s, had become ramshackle. The oldest building, constructed in 1860 in a distinctive Italianate style, would eventually house the Philadelphia Girls Rowing Club. Originally, it was the headquarters for a skating club, reflecting the popularity of ice-skating on the Schuylkill as a winter activity. Collectively, the boathouses comprise one of the more dramatic historic architectural landmarks in Philadelphia.

The past is all around you as you walk along Boathouse Row. You marvel at the distinctive nineteenth century architecture of the boathouses and the bustle of rowers arriving and departing. History saturates each building. Punctuating the aura are the balconies, turrets and towers that grace most of the buildings. Their flags, bearing club colors, fly triumphantly alongside Old Glory. Many of the boathouses have stacks of rowing shells along their outside walls because their inside bays are full. The stacked shells constitute strong hints of the activities within the buildings.

Those fortunate enough to gain entrance to any of the boathouses experience immediate history lessons, thanks to hundreds of framed photographs of successful past crews, and trophies, many of them tarnished with age. On the walls hang wooden oars with past victories recorded on their blades. Smells are ever-present in an unmistakable mix of old wood aroma, modern lubricants, paint or varnish, and just plain sweat from legions of rowers. .

In its way, visiting Boathouse Row is akin to a visit to the Vatican in Rome or to an old cathedral in France. Every sense is immediately aware that many important events took place here and that they all involved the male gender. There is nothing feminine about the physical appearance of Boathouse Row. These are buildings built by strong men and then used by strong men. Every square foot of them conveys that message. There is nothing feminine about their looks or the atmosphere they convey.

A second impression of Boathouse Row, gained after only a few conversations with club rowers, is that these buildings are staging areas for a highly competitive group of men who share legacies of hundreds of races rowed, hundreds won and hundreds lost. Rowing has always brought them together. But there are differences because each boathouse can boast of its own distinctive personalities who have shaped them. Historian and rower Joe Sweeney points out that Undine attracted rowers of German descent; Penn AC, his club, was for the Irish; the

University Barge Club is populated by Ivy League types; and Fairmount is blue collar, drawing rowers from the immediate Boathouse Row neighborhood, many of them of eastern Europe extraction.

He emphasizes the fact that the clubs have always been competitive. "In the earlier days we couldn't travel so much, so the clubs had to compete against each other," he said. "That's just the way it was."

This, then, was the culture that Ernestine Bayer challenged when she was twenty-eight years old. She knew it well by virtue of her marriage to Ernest Bayer, a prominent rower and, indeed, a man of the rowing establishment. Because of the associations made through her marriage, she was totally aware of the Boathouse Row culture as well as one of its primary dictates: Women did not row and were only welcome in the boathouses for social occasions.

Ernestine Bayer, age 30, June 1939   National Rowing Foundation

CHAPTER 4:
THE PHILADELPHIA GIRLS ROWING CLUB AND ITS FIRST RACE

Ernestine Bayer, in bow at left, and her partner, Jeannette Waetjen, wave in triumph after winning the first women's double sculls race ever held on the Schuylkill on July 16, 1939. The women's races that day "forever ended the male domination of rowing on the Schuylkill," Philadelphia Inquirer reported. National Rowing Foundation

ERNESTINE STEPPACHER MARRIED ERNEST BAYER, A BANKER, on Jan. 28, 1928. She was eighteen, he was twenty-four. At the time of the wedding, Ernest was a serious contender for seats on a four without cox as well as four with that were to enter the Olympics. Ernest feared disqualification if his marriage became known, since coaches and other athletic professionals of that era believed that sex sapped the strength of athletes. The couple decided to keep their marriage a secret.

A few months after the wedding, he was selected for the 1928 Olympics. His boat, the four without, won a silver medal that summer, losing the race by a mere foot to Great Britain. That loss haunted him for the rest of his life. Never again, Ernie recalled, did Ernest drink tea, the Brits' favorite drink.

Not surprisingly, Ernestine, always the athlete, and always a bit of a rebel on the issues of how women should behave, decided early in the marriage that she, too, wanted to row. Many years later she chronicled those feelings that later inspired her to reach out to other women with the idea of starting their own boat club. "Every day after work, May through October, for the first ten years of my marriage to Ernest Bayer, we walked to Boathouse Row in Philadelphia," she wrote. "While he spent time on the river, I would sit alone on the porch of the Pennsylvania Barge Club. The oarsmen and rowing officials, just as they do today, liked to party. I was an outsider, but also an insider through my marriage. I enjoyed the company and I had always enjoyed competition. Why should this sport be denied to women? I kept asking myself. There were certainly no opportunities for women in these clubs. Why then, shouldn't there be a rowing club for women?"

At first, she floated the idea gently among the men in the club, but also began to figure out how she could make it happen. She soon found that several very powerful men in the rowing community were dead-set against women getting a foothold on boathouse row. Their apparent leader was a rower named Henry Penn Burke.

Not being shy, Ernie asked him repeatedly, "Why don't women row?"

And just as repeatedly, Burke answered, "Women don't row, and furthermore there is no place for women to row from."

The notion that women didn't row was laughable, Ernie thought. She knew there could be a place to row from if there were a building available. And, in fact, there was one. For many years it had housed a skating club. She learned the building would be available through her job at the Fidelity Trust Company in Philadelphia. Raymond Parker, one of the bank officers, was also a member of the Philadelphia Skating Club. Parker knew that Ernest was involved in rowing, and that Ernie wanted to row. One day he mentioned to her that the skating club building on Boathouse Row was available for rent because the club had just built a new facility.

A few weeks later, an event happened that changed Ernie's life. As usual, she was sitting on the porch of the Pennsylvania Barge Club watching the men row. She spotted a woman coming out of the nearby Fairmount Rowing Club and getting into a single. Astonished, she watched the woman row away. Later, she discovered her name was Lovey Kohut, a nurse, who rowed as her work schedule permitted, which was why Ernie had not seen her previously.

On the way home that afternoon, she confronted Ernie, her husband. "You told me women don't row," she accused him.

"They don't," he said flatly.

"Well, I saw a girl taking a single out of Fairmount, and if she can row, why can't I?" Ernie demanded.

"She is rowing her boyfriend's personal equipment," replied Ernest. "You and I don't own a boat."

The situation was dicey, recalled Ernie. At the time, Ernest was captain and coach of the Pennsylvania Barge Club. She realized later that he had the authority to permit her to row one of the club shells, but he had not wanted to create a controversy that might cost him his job, even though it was an unpaid position, and his standing in the rowing community.

That incident made her determined to pursue the idea of a rowing club for women using the abandoned skating club

building. She spoke to Raymond Parker, her bank officer
and friend, and he arranged a meeting between Ernie and
club officials. Her daily lunch partner, Jeanette Waetjen, then
seventeen, who was also interested in rowing, joined her. There
was extensive conversation, but the president of the skating club
agreed to rent the facility for use as a rowing club.

Jeannette later described to Ernie her behavior at that
meeting. "Ernie," she said, "You talked yourself deaf, dumb, and
blind."

"I don't care," Ernie replied. "It worked."

She and Ernest socialized with members of Fairmount. One
of the men was dating Gladys Hauser, Ernie's coworker at the
bank. Ernie suggested that Gladys approach the other girls who
were dating Fairmount members to see whether they might be
interested in rowing.

Jeannette Waetjen, now Jeannette Hoover, a widow in her
eighties who still lives in Philadelphia, recalls that she was
two years younger than Ernie and that she had just joined the
Fidelity Bank as a messenger.

"It was during the Depression. I had graduated from high
school in February 1938 and would be seventeen in June. I was
just fortunate to get the bank job. I knew I couldn't go to college
and the banks needed messengers because telephones were not
used for calls between people within the bank.

"Anyway, Ernie sent a message around asking whether any
of the women wanted to row. I was the only one to respond. She
was married, and I had to keep it quiet because married women
were not supposed to work."

Ernie just kept talking about the idea of a women's boat
club, she said, and gradually some others became interested.
Ernie organized a founders meeting at her husband's boat club,
the Pennsylvania Barge Club, and, according to an account in

the May 8, 1938 *Philadelphia Record*, "...they were secretaries, saleswomen, nurses, models, typists, and just plain ladies of leisure." Some had had previous sports experience in basketball, bowling, tennis, and bicycling, but most had not, the article continued. Ernestine was described as "the attractive dark-haired wife of an Olympic oarsman."

On May 4, 1938, seventeen women met for the first time. They had heard Ernie speak about her dream of women rowing. They decided to rent the building, and then agreed to assess themselves dues of $25 a year, plus a $5 initiation fee. The first practice was to be May 14. They named the group the Philadelphia Girls Rowing Club and elected officers. Ernestine Bayer was the first president.

Founding members were Ernestine Bayer, Doris Starsmore Brugger, Sally Greeley Cibort, Lenore Mongan Davis, Lovey Kohut Farrell, Betty Flavin Ford, Kay McFarland Gillen, Jeanette Waetjen Hoover, Mary Prior Jonik, Helen Muldowney Kiniry, Gladys Hauser Lux, Eileen Coughlan Mockus, Lucille Browning Nino, Jeanne Murphy Quirk, Ruth Adams Robinhold, Marge Cantwell Sonzogni and Betty McManus Wilkins.

The first officers were Ernestine Bayer, president; "Sis" Cannon, vice president; Ruth Adams Robinhold, treasurer; Gladys Hauser Lux, secretary; Lovey Kohut Farrell, captain; and Mary Prior Jonik, lieutenant.

The newspaper account of that meeting said the club decided that the club would not sponsor races longer than one-half mile, "to satisfy those who are afraid that rowing is cruel for girls." At the time the standard race course was three-quarters of a mile.

All hell, or so it seemed, broke out on Boathouse Row, Ernie recalled. Many men were angry at having women invade their territory. Some of the Bayers' longtime rowing friends shunned them. In the early days, only a few men at Fairmount and

Crescent, another boat club, cautiously welcomed the women.

One man took Ernest aside and in a voice of grave concern asked him why he allowed Ernie to row. "My wife rowed once and got tuberculosis and died. Do you want that to happen to your wife?" he asked.

Ernie recruited both her husband and Tom Curran, an international-class oarsman, to teach the women to row, and Rusty Callow, a friend of the Bayers, was the coach. Fred Plaisted, a famous professional oarsman from the late 1800s, approached Lovey Kohut, the captain, and donated two old boats, the first of many cast-offs they would gratefully accept.

The charter members were well aware of male opposition to what they were doing but were somewhat relieved that it wasn't open warfare. Mostly, said Hoover, the men ignored them by turning their backs to the young women to avoid an encounter, or by not offering to help at times when help, or a little coaching, would have been welcomed.

There were occasional unpleasant remarks. The bow oarsman of a four that was passing the PGRC shell yelled, "You shouldn't be on the water…you should be home making babies!" Reportedly, that remark came from the father-in-law of one of the women rowers.

Ernie said none of the male rowers was personally unpleasant to her, perhaps out of respect for her husband, who was an active and respected member of the rowing establishment. However, she said, she knew they were not welcome on the river because people would tell her of incidents. For instance, she said, she welcomed two young nurses to the club who wanted to row. But they only stayed three weeks.

"They came to me and said 'Ernie, we have to leave the club.' I asked them why and they said that their boyfriends didn't think girls should row and they should quit."

There was another problem. Press accounts of the new rowing club, while welcome, did not help the situation. For instance there were full page photo spreads depicting the novelty of attractive women rowing in their shorts.

One account said that the men, many of them Olympians, accustomed to seeing their rowing achievements trumpeted, now saw those same achievements diminished to a paragraph, crowded out on the sports pages by photos of women rowing. Furthermore, the women had to put up with male rowers sneering at the PGRC as a "marriage club," asserting that the women were not there to row, but only to attract husbands.

"The grumbling, the opposition, always came back to me," Ernie said. "I was abruptly shunned by longtime friends and acquaintances. But it didn't matter. Not one whit."

In later years, she would give credit to her husband Ernest, who was caught in an uncomfortable situation. He was part of the old culture that his wife had challenged. He lost friends but became a great supporter, even taking on the responsibility of teaching the members of the Philadelphia Girls Rowing Club how to row.

"Sure, I accomplished a lot," Ernie recalled in her later years. "But I could not have done it without my husband's support. I was headstrong and put him in a tough position. He didn't like it, but he came through, and we could not have done it without him."

Ernest Bayer was the PGRC's first coach. However, he did more than teach. He also borrowed a training barge from the University of Pennsylvania. In the meantime, Ernie had recruited Fred Plaisted, the former world sculling champion, by then eighty-nine, to coach. Plaisted was old, but he was an imposing figure of manhood, six feet tall and 185 pounds. And, he had impressive credentials: In his long career, he had rowed more than 400 races in the US, Europe, Australia, and the Orient. Then he had coached for fifteen years at Bowdoin, Yale, Harvard, and Columbia.

Ernestine was among his students. She was captivated by the discovery that rowing really did meet all of her expectations. It wasn't just another sport. Instead, it was special. Each time she was in a shell, her feelings became more intense. In rowing, she found a metaphor for life. This medium of water, body, and boat brought together all of life's elements: power, delicacy, adversity, discomfort, disappointment, thrills, and the rush of speed.

On most days, these emotions were a mix, manifesting themselves in good strokes and bad strokes. On other days, everything fell into place and she was in a zone, with all aspects of her persona in harmony. Then there were the days when everything fell apart and she had to fight the weather, the water, and her own unresponsive body. But even on those days, she was secure in the knowledge that she had put it all together on at least a few occasions and could do so again. It just wasn't going to happen that day.

From her first halting stroke, Ernie knew that she had fallen in love with rowing and that some force compelled her to spread that love, no matter what. Often that love was not gentle; instead it manifested itself as a passion that was to continue for the rest of her life. The overwhelming force that she had begun to experience brought her persona into such sharp focus that, unwittingly and unintentionally, she often made other people uncomfortable, because she had focus and goals and they did not. She never could understand when other people failed to share her vision.

From the first stroke, the die was cast. Never again would her life be the same. However, as for so many other rowers, her first experience in a shell fell far short of being a piece of poetry.

In a newspaper interview some year later she recalled her first time in a shell. "I literally rowed in a circle," she said. "I still don't know how I did it. But there were a lot of boys on shore, laughing. And the madder I got, the bigger the circle I rowed in."

Ernestine, 1928   National Rowing Foundation

Notwithstanding, within weeks after first experiencing the rapture of shell and water, she bought a single so she could row on her own schedule without having to wait for a shell or crew. Every day after work, May to October, she rowed for an hour, longer on weekends. "I loved rowing from the start," said Ernie. "In rowing I discovered the many physical, emotional, and aesthetic joys that motivate athletes. But there was another result. I'd have to say the most profound change for me after I discovered rowing was that we ate out every night. I didn't have time to cook."

Those feelings became even more intense as she reached her senior years. "Rowing," she told *Boston Globe* writer Peter May when she was in her eighties, "is the combination of water, using your body, and looking at nature. When you see Fred Astaire and Ginger Rogers, you see rhythm. Rowing, to me, is rhythm. I've never thought of other sports as having so much rhythm. ... When you do it right, it's gorgeous."

A few years later, having reached her nineties, she still rowed, much to the astonishment of her friends. She continued to express what the sport had done for her. "It defined my being," she said. "Rowing became my way of life."

The PGRC's first race was on July 16, 1939. It was the first time in the US that women had competed in an exclusively female race. A finale to the traditional Schuylkill Navy regatta, the historic late afternoon event prompted the *Philadelphia Inquirer* to proclaim that the race "forever ended the male domination of rowing on the Schuylkill."

The story gave great credit to Plaisted and his rowers, reporting, "Under Fred's guidance they built up their arm and leg muscles, took weight off, inhaled tons of fresh air, and quieted jumpy nerves."

For Ernestine that first race on the Schuylkill was a triumph. She and her eighteen-year-old partner, Jeanette Waetjen, her friend from the bank, won the doubles event.

The half-mile race was filled with incidents, according to the *Philadelphia Evening Bulletin's* account. "Three crews competed, and in a sensational finish, they (the Bayer-Waetjen shell) were ahead by only a few feet when one of the rival combinations seemed to have their signals mixed and then, after their oars clashed, stopped rowing for a moment. The other rival crew steered so poorly that they were far astern.

"All of the crews were composed of members of the club, which incidentally was formed fourteen months ago, and whose members have been wishing, hoping, and praying for races ever since."

The article then took a swipe at the men's crews. "With the girls making their rowing debut, the other series of close races faded into the background in the regatta, which was the third of the Schuylkill Navy's match events."

Despite the triumph of the Bayer-Waetjen shell, that race was chaotic. As in so many other races by so many other rowers, they won not because of their skills but because of their opponent's mistakes.

The *Bulletin* story continues, "Victory by the Waetjen-Bayer duo was a fitting debut for the girls, although it was heartbreaking for Lovey Kohut, the 170-pound Hahnemann Hospital night nurse, and Stella Sockolowska, a young stenog, who had led by more than a length a quarter-mile from the finish. In fact, they had the race within their grasp until about 50 yards from the finish line, when they seemed to get their signals mixed or something.

"Oars clashed. One pulled and the other didn't, both stopped rowing, then started again. They were back in rhythm. But it was too late. Maybe not! They didn't give up without a fight, but the Waetjen-Bayer crew was winner by three feet, timed in 3.33.35 for the half mile and Kohut-Sockolowska in 3:34.15.

"Ruth Adams, a milliner, paired with Betty Flavin, a stenog, couldn't seem to keep the boat going in a straight line. They rowed from one side of the river to the other, and back again, and were far behind the leaders at the finish for third."

The *Philadelphia Inquirer* account was much more condescending. Under the headline "Six Rowing Maids Compete on River," the story reported that in the final minute of the race, "the winner's boat was on the inside of the No. 4 lane, but for a moment it looked as if they would crash into a wall. They straightened their course and then rowed smoothly at 26 strokes per minute ... slow for oarsmen but pretty good for the fair sex."

It continued, "The third pair, Betty Flavin and Ruth Adams, another 125-pound combination, stuck to the middle lane so closely that they nearly bumped the referee's motor launch which was busy steering clear of the young ladies."

The story's final paragraph damned the women with faint praise.

"However," it concluded, "the oarswomen members of PGRC deserve a big hand for their efforts. They did their best and no one fainted from exhaustion or went into hysterics."

Jeannette Hoover, then Waetjen, said that Stella and Lovey were stronger women and heavier than she and Ernie. It was very windy, she said, and she and Ernie could barely make headway in the first few minutes of the race because the wind blew them around, affecting their performance to a much greater degree than it affected their heavier opponents.

"I was stroke," she explained. "We made a quick decision to change course and head off at an angle towards St. Peter's Island where the water was calmer. We rowed a longer distance, but that move saved us because the wind died down once we were close to the island."

That race, however it was won, would be one of many firsts for Ernestine. She readily admitted that rowing for women took a long time to catch on. In the early years, the only races the Philadelphia Girls Rowing Club could get were the ones from within their own ranks. It wasn't until sometime after World War II that there was outside competition, and that came when a high school crew from Shrewsbury, Massachusetts, was persuaded to make the trip to Philadelphia, to compete against the local club.

The *Philadelphia Record* took note of the lack of competition in a story with photos on June 25, 1939. The headline read, "All Trigged Out in Rowing Togs and No Place to Go." The story then reported, "Rowing is fine fun, they agree, and good exercise, improving the posture and carriage … but it's depressing to haul out sculls, gigs, and what not and row them aimlessly on sleeveless errands leading to nowhere and back. … They want to race someone, somewhere, sometime…"

The problem was not only lack of competition, and lack of support from the male rowing community, but also lack of money.

The story continued, "Boathouse Row sniffed when the club was formed and so did all the Schuylkill Navy. They said it wouldn't last long and that girls weren't cut out for such strenuous exercise and all that.

"Well, the members (some 40 pay dues regularly) have trained faithfully for more than a year under the direction of Fred Plaisted, 90-year-old rowing veteran and his aides. ... They could enter the New England Regatta on July 9 but it takes money to send shells to New England. ...

"The girls are mostly 21 to 25 and most are saleswomen or clerks. The only married woman is Ernestine Bayer. They also have good equipment: five shells, a University of Pennsylvania 16-oar training barge, two doubles, a four, and a single ..."

In 1939, Ernie was thirty years old.

Philadelphia Girls Rowing Club, April 2006   Lew Cuyler

CHAPTER 5:
TINA AND
THE POSTWAR YEARS

*Tina Bayer graduation photo, May 1963 Mount
Saint Joseph's Academy, Flourtown, PA*
Bayer Family files

TINA BAYER CAME INTO THE WORLD ON SEPT. 30, 1945. Ernie's rowing hardly skipped a beat during her pregnancy. She continued to row right up through her seventh month, and was back on the water almost immediately after the birth. In fact, three weeks after Tina's birth, Ernie successfully defended her club singles championship.

The years between Tina's birth and the 1960s, when Ernie elevated women's rowing to national status and then international competition, were ones of relative quiet in an otherwise eventful life.

Although Ernie's enthusiasm for the sport was unabated, World War II had dampened rowing activity. "Boathouse Row was like a morgue during the war," said Jeannette Hoover. "Everything stopped. There were a few older rowers on the water and a few very young rowers, but that was about it. Everyone else was either off to war or engaged in war-related activities such as the 'Bundles for Britain' clothing drives, blood drives, victory gardens, making bandages, and other volunteer support activities."

When the men came back after the war it was different, she observed. Rowing had lost its momentum and the men had lost four years out of their lives. It would take some time for men's rowing to regain its momentum, and women's rowing activity really had to start all over again. Except for the hive of activity that Ernie had started at PGRC, women's rowing remained very limited.

Yet, Ernie continued rowing singles and doubles out of the PGRC, an activity she combined with the crowded schedule of being a mother, helping her elderly parents at their card and gift shop and tending to their other needs, and taking care of the family dog, Rebel. Several other women also continued the sport, with coaching provided by Ernest Bayer. Tina remembers that frequent boathouse visits were part of her childhood, as well as going out in the coach's launch with her father or with referees.

Racing was primarily confined to the dozen or so women at the PGRC, although at some point a double arrived from Minnesota to challenge Ernie and her partner Stella Sockolowska. They lost the race, an unheralded event, but one of only a few races in her life where Ernie did not triumph.

In 1956, the PGRC accepted an invitation to compete against Florida Southern College in Lakeland. Ernie put together a boat of herself and much younger oarswomen who trained all winter for the race. While still in Philadelphia, however, one of the PGRC oarswomen questioned whether the shell could be really competitive with Ernie, at age forty-seven, rowing in the seven seat. The coach, Tom Curran, dismissed the question, stating that Ernie was the best rower in the shell. In fact, the PGRC did lose, but only by one second.

Recalling her childhood years, Tina said that her mother was pretty basic in her tastes for food and interior decoration. She was very straightforward, preferring meat and potatoes to fancy foods and sauces. She liked to buy antiques, but was quite particular in her purchases. She kept a neat but simply furnished house. Her one weakness was for candy.

"She loved chocolate," her daughter said. "Her uncle was a candy manufacturer. My mother could take a whole box of chocolate Easter eggs and eat them at one sitting. She was capable of eating a whole five pound box of candy in a weekend. To this day, she loves candy."

Her love for candy, however, did not affect her looks. With her high cheekbones, flashing eyes, and trim athletic figure, it came as no surprise when she accepted a job in the mid-1950s as a Philadelphia model for mature women's clothing. After a few months, however, she discovered a dislike for the politics and pettiness of the profession and resigned.

"It just wasn't her cup of tea," Tina said. "She was good-looking in a natural way and did not like to spend a lot of money on clothes. The modeling agency wanted her to be dressed to the nines at all times, and even wear false eyelashes. It all made her uncomfortable."

One facet of her mother's personality was very clear to her even when she was a child, she said. "Mom has a very high energy level. She keeps going when others would stop. I don't think she ever took a nap."

58

Other women in the PGRC did not share that high energy level. As a result, by the late 1950s competitive rowing at the PGRC had all but died. Ernie rowed intermittently for pleasure but as the 1960s began, it was obvious that the club had lost its original zest. In fact, it had become such a non-entity that the men's clubs wanted to take over the space to accommodate the expansion of their rowing programs. The result was that in 1964, the City of Philadelphia threatened to revoke the club's charter on the grounds that it no longer offered a formal rowing program.

When Ernie heard about what could happen, she vowed to take action. She and Lovey Farrell, one of the original members, immediately called the other original members. The women met, voted themselves into office, and elected Ernie captain of the club.

Within a few months she had recruited Ted Nash, a two-time Olympic gold medalist in rowing, who was later to become one of the top coaches in the nation, to take over as coach. Somewhat surprisingly, in view of the times, he accepted. His then-wife, Aldina, was a club member, but even so, prospects for the club's rescue were far from certain.

Tina, who celebrated her fifteenth birthday on September 30, 1960, was coming into her own as a woman and as an athlete. She began swimming at the age of nine and then swam competitively in the high school league.

"Even though I grew up in a rowing family I never tried it because I was just too busy," she recalled. "Between swimming, being a top student at high school, and having a weekend job at a hairdresser's, I didn't have time. To stay on top, I just had to spend every minute of my spare time studying."

The turning point came one night when she was nineteen. Ted Nash had just agreed to coach the PGRC, and Ernie had invited him to dinner to discuss available women rowers at the PGRC. Like a dutiful daughter Tina was clearing the table, and was walking through the door from the dining room to the kitchen. All of a sudden, she heard him say, "Take your daughter, for instance. ... You think she is big and strong but she's not big and strong enough to row in one of my boats."

"I was mortified," Tina recounted. "All you have to do is say something like that to a nineteen-year-old who fancies herself a pretty good athlete and it's like the fur goes right up on her back. I was challenged, so the next day I said to Mom, 'When you go down to the club this weekend I want you to put me in a boat and teach me how to row.'"

"She did," Tina said. "She put me in a wherry."

The standard way to teach was for Ernie to lie down on the dock and hold the stern while she instructed. Tina had seen her teach new rowers this way for the past five years. But this time she played a trick, telling her daughter, "I can't hold on you to any longer. I am going to have to let you go, so just go up to that bridge," a reference to the Girard Avenue bridge, about one half mile upstream from the PGRC dock.

Ernie then released Tina's boat.

"Well," said Tina, "I thought she meant the Columbia Avenue bridge, which is much farther up the river, so I went underneath the Girard Avenue bridge and the second bridge right next to it and kept going. Still, this is my first time in a boat and I am catching a crab every other stroke and I finally told myself this was stupid. So I stopped and thought about the feather and the square, and then took five strokes with one oar and then five strokes with the other oar, and then tried it with both. And it was beginning to work, and I was telling myself, 'This is okay.'

"I finally turned around and rowed back, getting the hang of it with every stroke. As I came within shouting distance of the girls' club, I heard my mother yell, 'Have you seen my daughter, Ernestine?'"

"'I am your daughter,' I shouted back."

When Tina returned to the dock, she found that Ernie was frantic with worry. When Tina had rowed away and then did not turn around, Ernie ran to her car. She drove up the river but never saw her daughter. She feared Tina might have capsized and she and her shell might have gone over the dam downstream from Boathouse Row.

"She asked me where I had been and I told her I had rowed up to the pink bridge and back." Her first row had been approximately three miles.

"And I didn't flip," she told her mother.

Ernie said, "You don't do that the first time in a boat."

Tina responded, "Why not?"

"Knowing what I know now, no wonder she was worried," Tina laughed. "Anyway, from that time on I was hooked. I knew I could row. I knew I could be good."

In the meantime, Ted Nash began recruiting women and Tina was among them. Ted's wife, Aldina, also helped and also became one of the rowers in those early eights. Ernie also recruited, and almost every night held rowing classes for novices at the PGRC dock.

Besides teaching novices to row, Ernie raised money to buy boats, through raffles and other events. Some of the new members did not want to sell raffle tickets. Ernie explained in no uncertain terms that selling raffle tickets was a condition for membership. Those reluctant new members changed their minds, and eventually, they raised about $7,500, enough to buy two new doubles.

Their first race was in June 1965 against Mills College of Oakland, California with a match between two eights and two fours. Ernie rowed at seat No. 4, Tina was at No. 5, and Aldina Nash at No. 6. The outcome was even: Mills nipped the PGRC by ten feet in the eight, thanks to its strong come-from-behind sprint in the last one hundred yards. PGRC won the four by better than a length.

It turned out that the results were not nearly as important as the post-race talk between the two coaches, Ted Nash at PGRC and Ed Lickiss at Mills. They were so enthusiastic about the potential of women's rowing that they thought it could only develop through the formation of a group dedicated to its nurture. The result was the founding of the National Women's Rowing Association was formed later that year. Ted Nash was its first president.

CHAPTER 6:
A TEDDY BEAR ON
GREEN LAKE

*Nancy Farrell, left, and Tina Bayer raise
Teddy Bear mascot in triumph after stroking
to first at the 1968 Women's National Regatta
on the Schuylkill in Philadelphia. Photo was
taken at finish line.* Bayer Family files

T O CELEBRATE ITS FORMATION, THE **NWRA** ANNOUNCED
the first National Women's Rowing Regatta, to be
held on Green Lake in Seattle in 1966. For the PGRC,
this development brought new life with goals. It all
happened so quickly that in the days leading up to that first
regatta, the spirit of the club was cooperative.

The PGRC women's eight was now a fact of life, and in place
was an enthusiastic, experienced, and skilled coach. However, a
trip across the country to Seattle for the first women's nationals
was an enormous undertaking. The oarswomen in that first
eight had seldom ventured outside of Philadelphia, and for

young women who worked in offices, or were students or young mothers, finances were always a problem. A more serious problem was that, because of business commitments, Ted Nash could not make the trip. They would be on their own. However, there was no turning back; they had not come this far to give up a goal that provided both excitement and inspiration. So they practiced five or six times a week and saved their money. In the process, they planted the seeds of determination to win the national title.

They did not have the resources to transport their own shell cross-country. Instead, they would rely on a boat that they would draw from the host club's equipment pool.

The draw was unlucky. It resulted in a double-hulled Pocock 8 used by the University of Washington men's freshmen heavyweight crew, and therefore much too large—and heavy—for the Philadelphia oarswomen. Their determination abruptly collapsed in despair.

"We were devastated; we were in tears," said Tina Bayer. "The boat was so heavy we could barely lift it. We knew there was no way we could be competitive in that boat.

"We had gone through so much to get out here," said Tina. "Each of us had paid her own way. Each had made her own sacrifice in time, effort, and money. This was going to be our only race, because we had no one to race against in the East. We came all the way out here, only to find we would row in a boat with the weight of concrete. You have no idea how heavy a double-hulled wooden Pocock is. You try to pick it up and it's like trying to lift a brick wall."

The Green Lake junior women's coach came to their rescue. His name was Frank Cunningham, he had been a rower at the Vesper Boat Club in Philadelphia where he had met Ernest Bayer.

He had anticipated the arrival of the PGRC crew, and came over to their boat to pay his respects.

Instead of faces reflecting the excitement of participating in the first women's nationals, he saw expressions of abject dejection. "What's going on here?" he asked.

Several women blurted out their disappointment.

Frank immediately took charge. "Let's get this boat rigged and see how well you can move it," he said. He pulled out his rigging tools and went to work. Forty-five minutes later the shell was ready to row.

"Take her out," he said, "and I'll join you in the coach-boat."

"He coached us a bit and we had a reasonable row," Tina recalled. "Not great, but okay."

At the end of the practice, Frank asked where they were staying. They gave the address of their motel and, to their surprise, he said he would be over at seven o'clock that evening for a meeting.

He arrived promptly with a Teddy Bear. The bear was dressed in the PGRC blue and white colors and held a miniature oar in its hands. He sat down on a bed and immediately launched into a pep talk.

"This bear is your mascot," he said. "You are going to get into that race in that heavy boat, and at some point during those 1,000 meters, one or more of you will tire and wonder whether you have any more strokes left. This bear has the strokes and it's going into the boat with your coxswain. You guys have nothing to lose. Show them what you are made of. Bring pride back to Philadelphia. Don't let the other shell beat you. You can beat yourselves much easier than the other boat can," he declared.

"I don't remember much about the race," said Tina. "We won, but I don't remember by how much."

No matter. The eight win was a triumph for the PGRC even if the other shells, the quad and the four, lost.

When she saw the Seattle double row, Tina concluded that it was a boat that could be beaten. She immediately recruited Nancy Farrell, who had raced in the four with only two months experience. The two women, Tina, sixteen, and Nancy, fifteen, made up their minds then and there to train in the double for next year's National Women's Regatta in Oakland, California in mid-June 1967.

Tina's rowing heritage, through her mother and father, was well-known. Nancy also had a rowing heritage. She was the daughter of Lovey Farrell, the former Lovey Kohut whom Ernie had seen rowing out of the Fairmount club on the Schuylkill in 1938. That was the sight that led her to challenge her husband on the issue of women's rowing, a challenge that later resulted in the founding of the PGRC.

Their decision to team up in a double when they returned to Philadelphia was doable. The PGRC owned two new Pocock doubles, purchased with the proceeds of fundraising raffles. The women who had sold the most tickets had the honor of naming the new boats. They were christened the Crusader and the "3 Bayers."

Trouble, however, was already brewing at the PGRC. Tina and Nancy Farrell, and Carol Schuller and Jinx Becker, the doubles teams committed to training for the second annual Women's Nationals, believed they had first priority on the use of the two new Pocock doubles. The magnificent wooden lightweight single, named the Rip Van Winkle, was reserved for Jinx Becker, who was also training in the single.

There followed the classic boathouse unrest. The committed

racers believed they should have the top shells reserved for them because of competition. Others in the club felt that they were also entitled to the best shells by virtue of paying their dues. In the background was the almost universal boathouse credo that novice and recreational rowers should not use the best boats because they were not experienced enough to avoid damage to expensive equipment. There were also the rigging problems that exist in every boathouse where there is competition.

It should be pointed out that rigging is important to experienced rowers. Speed depends in part on optimum leverage from the oar. Such leverage is achieved by adjusting the shell to the rower in various places: footstretchers to get maximum push from the legs, oarlocks for pitch of the blade through the water and height of the oar off the water, and other adjustments to the seat and the track. Rigging is an involved process requiring careful measurements and, in some cases, the use of levels. Re-rigging a single can take fifteen minutes or more; re-rigging doubles, fours and eights takes much longer.

In short, issues about rigging and shells prompt discontent, especially in clubs with few resources and little experience. In the meantime, the nationals had attracted many new members to the PGRC. But national competition meant the club had at least a dozen elite rowers who felt they were owed the exclusive use of the best boats.

The undercurrent of discontent led to a parting of ways between the club and Ted Nash. Ted basically wanted to keep his focus on the competitive rowing program; by now, there were too many recreational rowers who could not support that goal.

Again the club might have foundered. Coming to its rescue as volunteer coaches were John Quinn, a premier coxswain at the Vesper Boat Club, head coach, and Ernest Bayer, Tina's father and Ernie's husband, assistant coach. They set their goals on competing in the 1967 nationals in Oakland. Since winter had arrived and with it a substantial decrease in rowing activity, the membership discontent quieted.

The undercurrent of male disapproval continued. Liz Bergen, who joined the club in the mid-1960s, recalled, "The men would row past the dock as we were launching or putting the shell away and yell, 'Any of you girls know how to cook? How to make rice pudding?' They would often refer to us as a 'cheesecake matrimonial club,'" she said, "out there looking for husbands." Quinn remembers that, despite their wins the year before when the Women's National Regatta made its debut at Green Lake, the PGRC was not taken seriously on Boathouse Row. "We were just not encouraged to spend a lot of time at PGRC," Quinn said, referring to the prevailing atmosphere at Vesper, a club that was still basking in the victory of its eight at the 1964 Olympics in Tokyo. "Rowing as a mainstream sport for women still had not been accepted. When you went downstairs in the PGRC boathouse all you saw was old equipment. It was clearly a different world from the competitive men's racing clubs. Now it's mainstream, but it wasn't then."

Quinn, however, took the women seriously.

"I was a premier cox at Vesper; I had paid my dues, so it wasn't a big deal to coach them," he continued. "Nobody said anything. Just about every cox at Vesper was also a coach, so coaching a PGRC shell was just one more boat out there that I coached." And, since there was no ice on the Schuylkill during the winter of 1967, the competitive rowers could use the water all winter.

"If the PGRC women had been there just to have a good time, I would have been out of there in a minute," Quinn said. "But that wasn't the case. These girls were deadly serious. The Women's Nationals was still a new regatta. These girls trained hard and I am here to tell you that I pushed them hard. It was winter coaching and that meant bone-chilling wind and cold, but it didn't matter. They worked."

Winter rowing is always much more challenging because the cold numbs the hands, making it difficult to control the oar. In addition, splashes that land on exposed parts of their bodies make rowers feel as if they had been slapped by wet, icy towels. Rowers use various clothing combinations to ward off the cold, but even so, the chill is ever-present.

"Training started right after January first," Tina said. "We rowed, we ran, we lifted weights. Nancy and I decided we wanted to row a double, but the tilt was towards the eights, the premier event, the glory race. That was the race the club wanted to win in Oakland, and by the spring the eight had started to pull together, thanks to the coaching of Johnny Quinn."

Quinn said that one of his techniques that paid off was to take two of the women and put them in the men's boat he was coaching at Vesper, and also take two of the Vesper oarsmen and put them in the PGRC shell. This allowed the women to experience the feeling of rowing in a stronger boat that could move faster and force them to work more aggressively to keep up. Putting two men in a women's boat, he said, gave them a different feel and allowed them to concentrate more on their technique.

Quinn was just as serious about the way they handled the boat on land. "My motto is that if eight of you row it, then eight of you carry it," he said. "Before I came that had never been the case and it always took ten or twelve women to carry the boat. If eight women could carry their own boat to the dock it meant they had a terrific psychological advantage over their opponents who needed help in getting the boat down," he added.

Quinn did not know the Bayers particularly well when he began his coaching stint, but he was impressed by all of them. He reflected the sentiments of most the Boathouse Row personalities when he said, "You got one, you got all three. They were inseparable."

The family was very close-knit. By this time they had gained enough prominence on Boathouse Row to be called Momma, Poppa, and Baby Bayer. Since they were named Ernestine, Ernest, and Ernestine Jr. the nicknames eliminated the confusion.

Baby Bayer was clearly one of the better rowers, he observed. Her father, Poppa, was quiet, unassuming, and tremendously supportive. He saw to all the details that made boathouse operations run smoothly.

"Momma was the strong personality," he said. "She was attractive, her hair was blonde-silver and she was vigorous. If a boat was short one rower for practice she would jump in and hold her own, despite the fact that she was then nearly sixty years old, or thirty-five years older than the other women in the boat. She kept up, even though it was a little difficult for her sometimes. She also took in all of these kids as if they were extensions of Baby Bayer. She was a mother hen to all of them."

The upshot of the winter of coaching was that the PGRC entered an eight, a quad, a four, a double, a pair, a single, and a heavyweight wherry in the national competition.

Quinn did not accompany his crews to Oakland. "I took them as far as they could go," he said, "but I couldn't go to California. I was dating a woman who was to become my wife and that was a big factor in my decision to stay home."

Everyone agreed that Quinn had been a terrific coach and was responsible for transforming the women from rowers to oarswomen. "We won every race at the Nationals," Tina said, "and we did it with ten rowers."

Joe Henwood, then a second generation premier rower at Vesper who later married Penny Gibson, a member of the PGRC crew, said that Quinn "got them away from the dainty short strokes and taught them how to row, how to slap wood," he said. "That's why they won."

Ernie, ever the competitor, was beside herself with pride. Characteristically, she had already found out about international competition. On their return to Philadelphia, she said, "Let's take a crack at it. The European championships are in September."

At the time, her idea was an impossible dream to everyone else but her. But it happened.

CHAPTER 7:
ERNEST BAYER

*Ernest Bayer and silver medal won at 1928
Olympics in straight four*

Bayer Family files

I N MARKED CONTRAST TO HIS WIFE, ERNEST BAYER WAS quiet in his demeanor. In appearance he was considered handsome, and in personality he was regarded as a "gentle bear of a man." He was six feet two, had black hair in his younger years, and hazel-colored eyes.

An Olympic rower, he never sought the limelight, but he was always there to provide strong support for all rowing activities. These activities included the ones his controversial wife, Ernestine, had undertaken in her determination to break through the barriers of the male rowing environment.

Ernest most definitely was a man of the establishment. He joined the First Pennsylvania Banking and Trust Company in 1923, starting out in the stock room and retiring as vice president forty-six years later. In 1928, he was bowman in a straight four that won a silver medal in the 1928 Olympics, missing out on the gold by a mere foot. He continued to compete until 1936, trying out for the Olympics in 1932 and 1936. He then turned to coaching, and at various times in his life worked with crews from Penn Charter, a high school; Temple University; the Philadelphia Girls Rowing Club; and in New Hampshire, at Exeter Academy and the University of New Hampshire.

For many years he was treasurer of the National Association of Amateur Oarsmen, the oldest athletic organization in the United States, founded in 1872 as the governing body of rowing. He was president of the organization in 1958 and 1959, and then treasurer for forty-five years. He was a highly-respected referee for races. He was a co-author of the Rules of Rowing, and he was Commodore of the Schuylkill Navy. He also acted as official or team manager at many international competitions. However, he never was too proud or self-centered to do the little things—such as making sure the gas cans for the coach-boats were full—that make boathouses run and rowing possible.

"There's always detail work that no one else wants to do, and he would be the guy who would step forward and get it done," said Charlie McIntyre, one of the Boathouse Row rowers who knew him. "If Jack Kelly or anyone else gave him an unpleasant task to do, he would do it, with no questions asked. He was a big lovable guy, a good oarsman, and loyal to all the rowers and the clubs along the Row," McIntyre concluded.

Quiet and dignified, Poppa Bayer commanded enormous respect in the rowing and business communities. Admirers use the same words to describe his personality: patient, kind, gentle, smart, a good listener, and a great negotiator. His integrity was such that the old school oarsmen who were offended and angered by his wife's behavior simply would not broach the subject in his presence. Ernest Bayer had paid his dues many times over; if his wife was overzealous in promoting the ridiculous notion that women should row, then so be it. His demeanor and credibility were such that his wife's behavior was not a subject for discussion.

Ernestine Bayer is the first one to tell you that she could never have accomplished what she did for women's rowing had it not been for the support of her husband, Ernest. And yet they had such different objectives. She challenged the rowing establishment that he represented. How could a man of such traditional loyalties tolerate a wife whose activities on behalf of women provoked such outrage?

The answer is that he loved his wife and was extremely proud of her spirit and of her zeal. But he was not a man to be at the front of the barricades in a fight. Instead, he stayed in the background, unobtrusive and strong, a man whom everyone could, and did, depend upon to keep things running. And because it was Ernest who asked for help on behalf of the PGRC, that help was given, and often it was in the form of rowing shells and oars.

He was superb the way he handled the controversy over Ernestine's activities, said Jack Frailey, who served with him on the board of the National Association of Amateur Oarsmen. "I think their marriage was a textbook for marital success and harmonious relations between the genders. He did not withdraw from the battle. Instead, he supported her as much as he was able, and he respected what she was trying to do. He just was not an aggressive person...but he was not inactive either."

He also had great respect for her rowing. Tina recalls the story that one evening her mother, her father, and Tom Curran were rowing singles when the coach launch of the Penn Eight, also out practicing, started bearing down on them. Rather than rowing through the anticipated wake from the launch, all three scullers decided to stay ahead of the eight and they did so, even though the eight is a much faster shell. Later it was learned that the crew of the Penn eight was astounded that the three singles had stayed ahead of them but even more amazed to discover that one of the scullers was a woman. Ernestine was a talented rower who won both respect and encouragement from her husband.

Ernest Bayer died on Jan. 13, 1997 at the age of ninety-two. On May 10 of that year, rowers paid an extraordinary tribute to him by scattering his ashes on the Schuylkill River in a rowing farewell along Boathouse Row. The ceremony was the final event of the traditional Dad Vail Regatta, where he had been chief referee for four decades.

Shortly after Ernest's death, Frailey, in a sympathy note to the Bayers, wrote, "The many hours spent with him, mostly relative to the sport, were some of the finest I recall with anyone. He was a man for us all, of high sensitivity, great wisdom and fairness, and one who always found the humor in sometimes difficult situations—the very sort of pal you always gravitated to because he made you feel comfortable and warm. His magnetism was pervasive and is the type of real noble character so rarely encountered today."

Ernest's work was well-recognized with his selection to receive the NAAO's prestigious John Carlin Service Award, his recognition as an outstanding referee through the award of US Rowing's John Franklin cup, and his induction into the Rowing Hall of Fame for his outstanding contributions to the sport.

The Portsmouth (NH) *Herald* account of Ernest's induction commented, "He is what sport, no matter which one it is, is really all about. He has taken years of enjoyment from it and returned to it the most valuable of things—his time and effort to help it grow."

Perhaps Tina, his daughter, best summed up his persona when she said, shortly after he died, that he was a "fine arts coach—he saw things other coaches didn't see." Among the things he saw was that women could row.

However, in the late 1920s, the relationship that eventually spawned a rowing dynasty had to be kept a secret. Ernest was in serious training for the 1928 Olympics, and feared being kicked off the team. It was also considered bad luck to have a newlywed on the crew.

Ernie accompanied him to the Olympics, but as a cheerleader and not as his wife. "Today people would shake their heads in wonder at the secret union," Ernestine said in an interview shortly after her husband's death. "It was thought then that sex lowered a man's strength."

Bayer's crew was also on uncertain ground for Olympic competition because they had been unable to raise the money they needed, in those days a requirement even for the crew that had out-rowed all comers in the Olympic trials.

"When we got to the boat in New York, Avery Brundage (of the US Olympic Committee) wasn't sure that our rowing group would go because we hadn't raised enough money," Bayer later told the Portsmouth (NH) *Herald*. "How do you raise money in rowing? It's the only amateur sport we have." Brundage, a staunch supporter of amateur sports, relented, Ernest said, and his crew brought home a silver medal.

Interestingly, David Halberstam, author of "The Amateurs," a book about rowing in the 1984 Olympics, made the same point. He noted that rowing would forever remain an amateur sport because it was so "remarkably resistant" to the television camera.

As TV defined sports, it never could be glamorous, he said, and therefore could not command substantial financial backing, especially since TV cameras liked to focus on individuals and "except for the single scull, crew was a sport without faces."

As a result, he concluded that rowing "would remain an anomaly, an encapsulated nineteenth century world in the hyped-up twentieth century world of commercialized sport... Rowing is the only true amateur sport left," he had observed.

The 1928 Olympic races were held in Amsterdam, Holland, on the Sloten Canal, a waterway so narrow that only two boats could race at a time. Several heats were required to decide the finalists. Ernest Bayer was bowman in the four without coxswain, a critical position in such a race because he was responsible for steering as well as rowing. The semi-final race had been tough, he recalled in a newspaper interview, and the American crew had thought that their major challenger in the two-boat final would be the Italian crew. Instead, the Italians finished third.

"The Italians hopped us at the start and we just couldn't get by them on the narrow channel," he said. "It seemed that the Italian boat just wanted to stay in the middle. With five hundred meters to go, I decided to steer right for it, knowing that if the oars or boats touched, our boat would be disqualified."

It was a performance reflecting sheer guts. "In the final seconds, the Italians veered away and we dug in and beat them," he said.

However, the final proved to be an enduring disappointment. Great Britain had not been tested in a semi-final race because of the way the crews were sorted out. Instead it rowed in a "row-over," an event without competition meaning that they could enter the finals more rested than the US shell which had had such a tough semi-final.

In the final, the US shell was ahead of the Brits right up until the final 250 meters. The Englishmen then charged and won the race by a second. The American crew had to settle for a silver medal.

"We went into the tent to change clothes after the race and we all cried like babies," Ernest said.

In an interview late in her life, Ernestine said that the loss tormented her husband for the rest of his life despite his many other accomplishments within rowing. "He just never could get over it," she said. "He was an Olympian and his boat lost by a foot."

She said the loss was especially poignant because in his later life he gave up rowing, and most other physical activity, altogether.

They had moved to New Hampshire in the 1970s, and Ernie had rediscovered the joys of rowing in the Maine coastal waters in an Alden Ocean Shell. She wanted Ernest, then in his seventies, to continue rowing. She persuaded him to take one of the Aldens out with her and Arthur Martin, the designer of the wide-beamed open water shell. She was triumphant, but found that once on the water, Ernest had trouble keeping up with her and Arthur, even though they were rowing slowly. Nevertheless, it was a happy occasion, or so she thought. On their way home, she suggested to her husband that they might do it again.

"I am never rowing again," he declared, reflecting a dark mood of anger and despondence. She could not change his mind.

Later, she concluded that her husband "was an Olympian, and as an Olympian he couldn't stand the fact that his wife and the designer of an open water shell could out-row him. I did not realize it at the time, but we had unwittingly destroyed his pride."

Ernest Bayer died on Jan. 13, 1997. On May 10, 1997 his many admirers in the rowing community paid extraordinary tribute to him by scattering his ashes on the rowing course. The shell Tina and Ernestine used for occasion is antique double restored by Bruce LaLonde with support of University Barge Club. LaLonde is in bow of shell, Ernestine, in middle, is stroke and Tina, with back to camera, is coxswain. Bayer Family files

CHAPTER 8:
THE ROAD TO VICHY

Philadelphia City Business Men's Club presented contribution to PGRC oarswomen in late summer of 1967 to help defray expenses for their entry into World Regatta at Vichy, France in September. Presenting check is George Fay. Oarswomen, from left, are Marjory Pollock, Janet DuBois, Barbara DePena Hoe, Janice Saudargas, Tina Bayer, Faye Bardman, Jin Becker, Carol Schuyler, Penny Gibson and Nancy Farrell. Eight of the ten oarswomen in photo went to Vichy along with others who were absent when photo was taken.

Bayer Family files

TO FULFILL HER DREAM OF TAKING THE CHAMPIONSHIP **PGRC** women's eight to Vichy, France for world competition, Ernie first needed the official sponsorship of the National Association of Amateur Oarsmen. The revered, nearly-century-old organization set the rules and otherwise governed all rowing competition in the United States.

The world regatta was run by the Federation International des Societies d'Aviron, otherwise known as FISA, founded in 1892. Along with the NAAO, founded in 1872, and the Schuylkill Navy, founded in 1858, it shared a rich tradition of rowing. Unlike its American counterparts, however, FISA recognized female participation in rowing and had sponsored the European Women's championships since 1954.

Because the PGRC had won so many events at the 1967 US national women's championships, Ernie believed its eight had qualified to compete in Europe. Shortly after returning, she approached John Carlin, the North American representative to FISA who had the responsibility for signing the entry forms for US crews entering the FISA international competitions. A Philadelphia architect, Carlin was a carefully-dressed man of the establishment. His manner exuded leadership and total ownership of his role as arbiter of rowing in the United States.

Carlin thought her dream of competing in Europe to be absolute fantasy. Women's rowing programs were well-established in the European countries, he pointed out. Furthermore, the Soviet Bloc, which had a substantial number of crews, subsidized their programs to insure their excellence and thus proclaim to the rest of the world the advantages of the Soviet system.

The PGRC crew, Carlin asserted, was just not up to the mark. Instead, it would be sure to embarrass the United States, making it compare unfavorably to the Soviet countries. As the FISA representative in the US, he simply could not allow that to happen and therefore would not approve the entry.

Carlin, who died Nov. 8, 1968 at the age of seventy-two, commanded enormous respect in the US rowing community. At his death, *Rowing News*, the NAAO publication, said that he "was without doubt the most important single rowing executive on the American rowing scene for the past quarter-century. The breadth of his activities touched virtually every level of our sport, from the grass roots to the heady world of international rowing."

There was no question that he was an authority in the rowing world and that he had paid his dues. In contrast, Ernestine Bayer was a rank newcomer, an upstart, without a clue about international competition.

"You have to understand guys like John Carlin," said Joe Sweeney, the Boathouse Row historian. "They didn't like change. In their minds they were the defenders of our culture. They were the guys who carried weapons and fought our wars, and when they came back they demanded respect because they had undertaken enormous responsibilities, had made enormous sacrifices, and had otherwise put their lives on the line."

John Kiefer, now in his eighties and a close friend of John Carlin at the Fairmount Rowing Association, said that John had a deep and genuine interest in rowing. "He wasn't one to hold the girls back; there was nothing vindictive about it, he had nothing against women's rowing," he said. "He just knew that they weren't ready for international competition and had to act accordingly."

Ernestine was profoundly disappointed at his decision, especially since it left her powerless to do anything more. To race in Europe, she needed Carlin's approval. Those were the rules. Without that approval, she and club could look forward only to limited competition. Just as important, she was not accustomed to hearing the word "No." It wasn't part of her vocabulary. She did not understand its meaning.

She and Tina went to Carlin's house to discuss his decision. He offered tea and, in the ensuing conversation, Ernie asked him to reverse his decision because "the girls had worked so hard to earn this opportunity."

"Ernestine," he said, "four Russian women carry their eight down to the dock, and the other four carry the oars. It takes twelve of your women to carry the shell. That's a big difference."

Ernie's retort was immediate. "It takes twelve of us because we are using borrowed equipment," she said. "We don't want to take a chance of damaging the boat."

Then, a few days after the Carlin decision, there was an unexpected opening as if through a back door. At first, it did not even look like an opening. But Ernie saw the door open a crack and immediately put her foot in that crack.

Marjorie Pollock, now Ballheim, the cox of the PGRC women's eight, told Ernie that Craig Swazey, editor of the Toronto newspaper, was a friend of hers. He was very active in rowing circles, and unlike his US counterparts, he wanted to see a women's rowing program established in Canada. She and Ernie talked to him with the result that he invited the championship PGRC eight to participate in a "demonstration rowing race" against a men's eight of former Olympians. The race, with nothing at stake except for entertainment and publicity, was to take place at the First North American Rowing Championships, August 10–13 at St. Catherines, Ontario, Canada.

The regatta was to be a huge event. It had been in the planning for fifteen years and involved an excess of $2 million in expenditures. *Rowing News,* the NAAO publication, commented that it was "the most ambitious project in the history of North American rowing."

The article continued, "Originally designed to commemorate 100 years of rowing in Canada and mark the sport's participation in celebrations marking the Centennial of Canadian Confederation, the regatta will also introduce the country's new national rowing course while at the same time providing North America with its first FISA-sanctioned continental championship."

Ernie immediately saw the opportunity for her US championship women's eight and the PGRC. A race against former Olympic rowers would surely draw a large crowd, not only because of the Olympians but because of the women. The most important people in the rowing world would attend. She believed her rowers were good enough to win, and if they did, an enormous amount of publicity would follow.

She expressed these thoughts at a meeting of the rowers in the PGRC championship eight, and after several minutes of agonizing over the additional cost of traveling to Canada when they still had not paid off the expense of the trip to California, they said, "Let's go." This in itself was remarkable testimony. None of the women was wealthy. Instead, most worked in offices as secretaries or filing clerks and were paid accordingly. They also had vacation issues. Their decision meant that each would sacrifice more time, more money.

Pollock's friend Swazey recruited an eight of older rowers, including such former international champions as media-genic Thomi Keller, the glamorous Swiss-German aristocrat who was the current FISA president. At fifty, he was the oldest man in the shell. Although past their competitive prime, all of the rowers had medals testifying to their wins in world competition. The race was to be 500 meters, only one-quarter of the 2,000-meter Olympic distance. Put another way, it would be a high-speed sprint for the entire distance.

Tina Bayer, who was in the seven seat, said, "At the time, we weren't fully aware of it, but we had an advantage in such a small race because we were used to rowing together as a crew. The men were all great rowers but they had not rowed together. The result was we jumped them at the start and then kept rowing at full power because we knew we only had to go 500 meters.

"The men recovered almost immediately after the start and steadily gained on us. The finish was a dead heat, disappointing perhaps, but we were never expected to be that competitive," she said. "It was a huge surprise."

In the evening following the race, the Philadelphia women were invited to a party for referees, which included a host of rowing organizers from the various countries that belonged to FISA. Among them was Thomi Keller, the FISA president, who had rowed against them. He sought out the Bayer women, mother and daughter, to offer his congratulations.

Everyone knew Keller. He was dashing, handsome, multilingual, intense, and athletic. His stocky appearance and dark hair were eye-catchers. He had the reputation of being a ladies' man who had the ability to tell off-color jokes in English, French, and German without missing a beat. He was autocratic, running FISA "with an iron fist," as one observer put it. He had world presence.

And the PGRC's afternoon performance had impressed him. "If the race had been a travesty, he never would have made the move that night," said Joe Sweeney, the Boathouse Row historian who knew him.

"First of all, we were really flattered when he came over with his congratulations," said Tina. "Thomi Keller was the number one spokesman for rowing in the world."

Keller asked the Bayers about their next competition. Ernie told him that they would like to compete in the world competition at Vichy, France, in early September.

"But," Ernie added, "it isn't going to happen."

"Why?" Keller, surprised, wanted to know.

"First, our rowers don't have the money to go; second, we haven't trained; third, entries just closed; and fourth, which is the biggest roadblock, John Carlin won't okay our application," Ernie told him.

Keller then looked her straight in the eye. "Ernestine," he said, "you take care of the money. I will take care of John Carlin." Tina asked when the entries closed.

"In five minutes," he said, "but I will give you until midnight. Here are the forms."

With Keller watching, Tina and Ernestine immediately filled out the entry forms. He took them over to John Carlin. Without protest, Carlin signed them.

"When Keller said he wanted something to happen," Tina observed, "it happened. That's all there was to it."

Ernie then wrote a check on money the club didn't have, and handed it over to FISA for the entry fee. The PGRC had just entered the world regatta with a quad and an eight.

Word spread to the crew members. A celebration meeting was quickly called. The women gathered in one of the PGRC's hotel rooms.

Five wanted to go to Europe and four did not. They did not have the money. They were already in debt because of the trip to California and now to Canada. They had already made commitments for the balance of the summer.

Ernestine forcefully dismissed their concerns. "You will never have another opportunity like this in your entire lives," she declared. "You can be the first women's crew to represent the US in international competition. You can be number one in the world. This is your chance. Take it."

There were reservations, there was discussion, but in the end, their decision to go was unanimous.

As soon as the meeting ended, Ernestine sought out a man

named Horace Davenport, a man she had seen at the party. He had founded the National Rowing Foundation the year before to provide financial support for competitive crews. She was certain that he either had the money or access to money to send her crew to Europe.

Davenport, who was popularly known as "Davy," had grown up in financially-constrained circumstances in Brooklyn in the 1920s and then had landed a scholarship to Columbia, where he went out for sports teams—football, swimming and crew—reportedly so that he could eat. In that era, there were training tables for athletes.

"Davenport's greatest success came in crew," The *New York Times* reported on Jan. 17, 1988. "He rowed for the last two Lion eights to win national championships, in 1927 and 1929 at the Poughkeepsie Regatta. Then he went into the world to make his fortune and did so, in coal and oil businesses.

"In the 1960s, Davenport rekindled his passion for rowing by founding the National Rowing Foundation, which raises money and invests in the sport…"

He also had the reputation of having a lot of "street smarts."

"He was the Godfather of rowing," said Ernie, "so it took a lot for me to screw up my courage to go talk to him in the middle of a social event."

However, she did. She told him the story of the PGRC national championship, she told him how the National Association of Amateur Oarsmen had refused its endorsement, but how Thomi Keller, just that night, had prevailed to reverse its decision. She told the story of a bunch of young secretaries and office workers who could row, and row well, but were without funds.

"I asked him to lend us $6,000 to send the girls to Europe, because the girls couldn't afford the trip," Ernie recounted. She told him they would pay back each month from their paychecks. "You will be repaid every cent in a year," she promised. Ernie's forcefulness, her convictions, her sense of opportunity were dramatically evident.

Seconds passed. Davenport was taken. He found himself unable to say no. He, too, had been a fighter. He knew where Ernie was coming from and could relate to her plight. Almost instinctively, he reached into his pocket, extracted his checkbook, and wrote a check for $6,000. However, he told her, "this gift has to be anonymous."

Ernie took her promise of a payback seriously. Each month following Vichy, she reminded her rowers of the debt. "It took a year of each one paying back a little bit each month from their paychecks," she continued, "and when I finally had it all I went back to Horace Davenport and presented him with a check for $6,000."

She recalled that a dramatic moment of silence followed. He then accepted the check and said, "Ernie, I never expected to be paid back."

Many years later, Marjorie Bullock, now Ballheim, reflected on the events of the evening. "Keller had respect for us after the race that afternoon," she said. "He knew, probably more than anyone else, the kind of competition we would face in Europe. He knew it was important for the US women to take that first baby step to get on the world stage towards the Olympics. He was powerful, influential, and he thought the PGRC deserved a chance. If it was going to be embarrassing, okay, but we should get the chance…And we didn't embarrass.

"Davenport," she said, "stepped up to the plate and helped push us through the door. He knew we didn't want the money just for a trip to Europe. He knew we were serious. He knew women's rowing was going to happen and he wanted to be the person to help make it happen. And, at that point, we were the best in the US."

For the women, the rest of the summer—only twenty-one days—was given over to rowing and working. There were two practices a day, one before the women went to work and one after work. Because of time constraints the women lived at the PGRC boathouse, bringing in sleeping bags and blankets. They set up a training table and cooked their own meals.

During those three weeks, Tina said, "we woke up, rowed, ate, went to our jobs, rowed, ate, went to sleep. In between, we did fundraisings to augment the money Mom had borrowed. We figured it would cost each girl $600, not much nowadays, but a lot then. We were all of different ages. Nancy was sixteen, I was twenty, Mom was fifty-eight and a spare. Some of us gave up vacation plans. Our total focus was Vichy."

The male rowers, in the meantime, took little notice of the women's activities. However, there was an unexpected last-minute truce in the war of the sexes on the Schuylkill. On the night before their departure, Ernest Bayer, who had been coaching them, suggested a final row in front of the cluster of boathouses.

The women rowed down the river and as they turned their shells around for the upstream row, they saw the men on the porches of the boathouses unfurl banners reading "Good luck, PGRC."

"It was a great send-off," said Tina.

"And I just cried and cried and cried," said Ernie. "We were being recognized…at long last."

CHAPTER 9:

<u>VICHY</u>

Oarswomen, parents, and supporters arrive in Paris to take train to Vichy where they
will be the first American women to row in international competition. Note uniforms
that they put together from various outlets and then sewed on the appropriate patches.
National Rowing Foundation

O STENSIBLY, THE FOCUS WAS ON THE PERFORMANCE OF
the US team, both men and women, during world
rowing competition in Vichy, France, that first week
of September in 1967, when the US oarswomen
made their first bid for international recognition. But in reality,
circumstances dictated that the women would be on their own
and would function independently from the men. The US
oarswomen may have gained official sanction from the US rowing
organization, but that did not mean they would be treated as
equals to the men's team at Vichy. The conflicting views about
women rowing in Philadelphia that had so roiled the Schuylkill
waters would endure at Vichy.

Nine women were to compete in the fours and eights. They were all of different weights and heights. Nancy Farrell, the stroke, was heaviest and tallest at 170 pounds and six foot two. Tina Bayer, 155 pounds and five foot nine, was No. 7; then came Penny Gibson, No. 6 seat, 165 pounds and six feet; Evelyn Bergman in No. 5 seat, five foot four and 160 pounds; Jinx Becker, No. 4, at 140 pounds; Janice Saudergas. No. 3, 140 pounds and five foot eight; and Barbara DePena at No. 2 seat, five eight and 140 pounds. Sophie Socha Kozak, 130 pounds and five foot two, rowed in the bow seat. After the race Kozak would reveal that she was two months pregnant.

They also had various occupations and it had been difficult for many of them to take the time off. Four of them, Jinx Baker, Sophie Socha Kozak, Janice Saudergas, and Penny Gibson were secretaries. Barbara DePena was a commercial artist. Evelyn Bergman worked for a local insurance agency. Tina Bayer had just graduated from the University of Pennsylvania, Marjorie Pollock was an assistant receptionist, and Nancy Farrell, the stroke, was a seventeen-year-old high school student. Liz Bergen, a spare, was a fourth grade teacher.

Ernestine Bayer was coach, manager, and spare; Ernest Bayer was coach.

Joe Henwood, a Philadelphian who rowed in the US eight and later married Penny Gibson, described the women as "really strapped. They had borrowed money, they made their own uniforms, they either quit their jobs or got fired for leaving for rowing competition," he said. "In contrast, the men had everything handed to them, including per diem and walk-around money."

The men had everything done for them because they were under the umbrella of the National Rowing Foundation. They had managers specifically allotted to the team to make the arrangements for their accommodations; they had coaches, trainers, and masseurs; and they stayed at a five-star hotel.

"We had to do everything for ourselves," Tina said. "Besides raising money, that meant sewing our own uniforms, transporting the oars we had borrowed, and dealing with the hotel people and restaurants."

Creating appropriate uniforms turned out to be a huge effort. Team members first went to a uniform supply house and bought washable white nurse's dresses with short sleeves. Over the dress they wore navy blazers. They sewed the USA crossed-oar patch on them as their identity. They then went to a discount shoe store and made a deal on navy blue pumps with small heels and navy blue over-the-shoulder pocketbooks.

In the meantime, Ernestine had found a Philadelphia wholesaler and had purchased eighteen navy blue and white scarves and red berets.

They all thought their ensembles looked pretty sharp. Their do-it-yourself effort was in sharp contrast to the men's team, for which the Olympic clothing was supplied.

They wore their outfits for the opening parade, outdressing their European counterparts who wore sweat clothes to the ceremonies. They did have sweats, however. They had gone to an Army-Navy store and had bought navy blue cotton sweat pants and white sweat shirts. Again, they sewed on the official patches.

Once they arrived in Paris, the team even had trouble getting to Vichy, whereas the men had the transportation arranged for them. The women were to discover that the first class train they had booked would not take the baggage of the oars they had borrowed for the regatta. With the baggage rejected, they then had to carry their oars from one side of the station to the other where they negotiated with several French rail officials. To their credit, the French eventually gave in and hooked the baggage car carrying the oars onto the first class train, a solution they had first rejected.

The French in Vichy, however, gave the women a huge and unexpected welcome.

"We were met at the train station by the Mayor of Vichy and we were dressed for the occasion, all of us in our red, white, and blue outfits," said Liz Bergen, the team's spare. "Then we took a shuttle to our hotel, but missed a stop and had to run to catch another. There were a few cries of 'Americans, go home' while we were running that were surprising, especially after our welcome. We didn't know what to make of that."

The French welcome, she said, was in sharp contrast to that given to them by the American men. She said the Philadelphia coach, Dietrich Rose, had told his crews not to talk to the women, "because we would be a distraction." Tina Bayer said he also told her mother to keep her girls away from the men's crews, again because they would be a distraction.

The result was that most of the US men rowers ignored the women, with the exception of the Harvard eight.

"Their oarsmen were allowed to talk to us," Bergen said.

Jack Frailey, one of the Philadelphia oarsmen, said, "No one ever meant to be a sexist and it was not a case of not wanting to look after them. But it was a case of not having the time. Stories about their lack of money, their fundraising efforts, sewing their own uniforms, getting lousy boats and accommodations, are certainly accurate. But the fact is that nobody had the time to care about the women."

The women's hotel, The Pyrenees, was comfortable, but did not have the space or the other amenities that the men enjoyed at their hotel, and the language barrier was difficult to overcome. They bunked two to a room, with the water closets down the hall. Tina Bayer had become the quasi-leader of the women because she was the only one who could speak French, although not sufficiently well to insure successful transactions.

The women asked for bottled water for brushing their teeth, since the local water was not considered clean enough to drink. Each received a bottle of Vichy mineral water, but when they mixed it with American toothpaste, the resulting bad taste was not only a surprise, they had to spit it out.

"Then I had to go down and explain in broken French and pantomime that their prized Vichy water was not fit to drink," Tina said. "It was highly embarrassing, but the message got through and from then on we had plain bottled water in our rooms."

The hotel did not serve meals, so the women sought a restaurant within walking distance of their hotel. Tina made a mistake: she forgot to take her French dictionary.

"So we picked out a restaurant and we walked in. It was eleven o'clock in the morning and there was no one there who could speak English. I managed to convey the fact that we had an entourage of eighteen people, including parents and coaches, and that we needed lunch."

The only menu words that Tina could make them understand were steak, potatoes, salad, and bottled water. "I negotiated a price and that was the meal we ate for the next six days," she said.

Breakfast was another problem. The hotel only served a *petit dejeuner* of croissants and coffee, not nearly enough energy-producing fuel for oarswomen in competition. The hotel people gave the women permission to use the kitchen for breakfast. Ernie, Mrs. Pollock, the mother of coxswain Marjorie Pollock, and another friend, Cathy Sader, cooked.

"As a result we had bacon, eggs, toast, juice, coffee, cereal, just as if we were at home," Tina said. "This was an extended training table…and one day when we were sitting down to eat, we discovered a few strange men sitting at our table. The US officials had discovered that the American women had figured out how to get a decent breakfast in Vichy."

As for women rowers, "Vichy showed us what was out there," said Marjorie Pollock, now Ballheim. She and the others were amazed at the physicality of the European rowers.

"When we saw the Bulgarian women, our mouths dropped open," said Liz Bergen, the spare. "They looked like they all were cut to shape by the same cookie cutter. They had immense shoulders and muscles you couldn't believe. They had huge upper bodies. It made us glad that we were still feminine-looking."

"I remember watching the Bulgarian women carry their shell," Tina said. "They were six one and six two. We thought they were all on steroids. All we could say was 'Ohhh' …We were competing against people who had an enormous advantage on us because they were cranked up on drugs, and we weren't. The only drug we ever took was beer."

Penny Gibson, now Henwood, who rowed in the six seat, was equally amazed. "Oh my God," she said. "The Bulgarian women looked like men. They had hairy armpits, and they were strong. They took their four and flipped it up over their heads as if it were a baton.

"The East Germans were tall, blonde, beautiful. They were disciplined. And they, too, looked like men. They shocked the hell out of me. Made me take a look at us and, well, we just looked like girls."

It was intimidating. They had never experienced international competition. They knew the Russians were a better crew. "One of the Russian rowers told me they went to warm countries in the winter to train," Penny Gibson added. "It immediately struck me that these girls don't work—they row. Rowing is their job. What a contrast! We were mostly office girls and some of us had lost our jobs because our companies wouldn't give us the three weeks off we needed to go to Vichy.

"However, we had fun. For us, rowing at Vichy was not a job. It was fun. It was a wonderful experience that I will never forget."

Five of the nine women rowers competed in both the quad and the eights category. Although they did not expect to medal, the first race in the borrowed quad turned out to be a profound disappointment. The five-woman US crew—four rowers and a coxswain—had never been defeated and was ahead of everyone else in the initial thousand-meter heat. Then a rigger broke. They lost power, and they could only manage a fourth. They were unable to have the rigger repaired in time for subsequent races, so they decided to drop out of the quad competition and concentrate on the eight.

By this time they had also found that they were really not prepared for world competition, despite the daily two-practice routine in August. The hiatus between the California nationals in June and the Canadian race in July had taken its toll. By the time they returned from Canada they had had less than four weeks of serious practice.

They also weren't ready for the start. The French start command is *"Etes vous pret?"* which translates to "Are you ready?" Then there's a short pause before the starter says *"Partez,"* meaning "Go."

The shells with experience in international competition started as soon as the announcer said "P'uhh" but before he completed *"Partez."*

"We made a mistake. We waited for him to say the full word and then we started. The other shells started on the 'P' and they immediately had a half-length jump on us," Tina said. "We just didn't know and it probably cost us the race at the start.

"I don't really remember the race," she continued, "I just remember rowing like hell and thinking that they were better than we were. We came in last, maybe twenty seconds out of first. We were all pretty discouraged after the race, especially because there were no other heats or *repechage*, since there were just not enough women's shells entered."

A *repechage* in rowing competition allows losers to continue the competition through heats so that they can qualify for the *repechage* final.

Penny Gibson remembers that, for awhile, the US women were ahead of the Czechs with about one hundred meters to go. Then the Czechs sprinted and overtook them just before the finish.

Tina Bayer remembers going to the locker room after they had racked their shell. "We were down on ourselves. We had hoped we would do better. We started to shower and change, and suddenly all these other women from the countries we had raced against came in. They wanted to trade shirts. What an important and flattering gesture, because rowers don't trade shirts with losers!"

The visitors were primarily from the Iron Curtain countries—East Germany, Russia, Bulgaria, and Romania.

"They were just so happy to have us there," Tina continued. "When they cleaned out our shirts, they went for the clothes off our backs. If you had blue jeans, they were worth an entire sweat suit. There must have been a hundred women in the locker room, and nobody spoke English but us. They even wanted our underwear. Even Dad joined in. He yelled to me, 'Don't give up your shirt—I got you a pair of shoes from Holland!'"

The effect of the post-race clothing exchange was profound. It meant that the European racing community had accepted the US women and that they were pleased at the opportunity to compete against them.

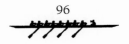

Rowing News, in its coverage of the competition, said that "the most unusual and perhaps in a way the most significant international competition by any US crew this year was by the Philadelphia Girls Rowing Club at the European Women's Championships at Vichy, France...

"Most of the girls are secretaries or students and most are around twenty-one years of age. ...They had no illusions. They were in over their heads and they knew it. Women's rowing is a major sport in Europe conducted at a fiercely competitive and highly competent level. Some European distaff eights can row their 1000 meters (standard women's distance) in 3:20 or better, a performance that is beyond the capabilities of many male junior crews.

"The results were anticipated. In the six-boat eight-oared final the US gals quickly fell behind their high stroking opponents and ran dead last. Still they rowed a most creditable race and even surpassed their own record breaking their national time set at Oakland.

"The favored Russian crew just edged East Germany by a quarter length in 3:14. Romania was third, nearly two lengths further back. The Netherlands finished fourth by another length. Czechoslovakia and the USA trailed by another 2 ½ and 3 ½ lengths.

"The Quaker City gals received a warm, generous welcome from their European rivals, who were both surprised and delighted at this unexpected American entry. The Russians especially greeted them most warmly and invited them to dinner after the racing ended.

"The comely Philadelphia gals, however, made good use of this opportunity to do some 'missionary' work among their male counterparts on the 'official' US team at Vichy. The Harvard eight especially became leaders of the Yank cheering section..."

The American oarswomen did not know it, but the European women regarded their presence as a leg up in their own aspirations to compete in the 1976 Olympics. An unnamed Dutch coach, who joined the celebration, reportedly told one of the rowers, "I hope you realize that your coming here will open the way for women to be in the Olympics in 1976."

At the time, neither that rower nor the other US oarswomen knew anything of the Olympics or Olympic politics. But it was clear that the PGRC's presence in Vichy had a much larger impact than the showing of just nine rowers. It was also apparent that competitive rowing for women in America had entered a new era. Rowing would never be the same.

The European experience had added fire to Ernie's enthusiasm. She told the *Philadelphia Bulletin* on her return, "I just get so excited about rowing. I just can't understand why more women don't row. It's great exercise and one that men and women both can participate in no matter their age. ...

"You can row up the river in several minutes or take all afternoon if you want. I still row about four times a week and help teach the new girls."

1880's rowing, a male only activity on the Schuylkill

CHAPTER 10:
<u>ERNIE</u>

Ernie: "Liberated because of rowing."   Bayer Family files

THE **PGRC** WOMEN'S EIGHT HAD PROVED TO THE world that American oarswomen were worthy of international competition and, on the surface anyway, their achievement was recognized and celebrated.

"Vichy gave us credibility on Boathouse Row," said Penny Gibson Henwood. "They realized that we weren't just a bunch of women looking for boyfriends."

Her reference was to PGRC's reputation along Boathouse Row in the mid-1960s as the "Philadelphia Matrimonial Society," a club the girls joined because it offered the opportunity to meet men.

Mary Colgan, the wife of a Vesper rower and therefore close to the Philadelphia rowing scene in the 1960s, said that as women's rowing developed "there were always two cliques in clubs, each with different goals—the social people and the rowing people."

For many years, she said, the PGRC had been "dormant" for the rowing people until "Ernie's vitality took charge again and made it back into a rowing club. Ernie had continued to row in the years after World War II when rowing virtually stopped, but raising a child and other responsibilities took her focus away from competitive rowing during the postwar years and through the 1950s."

Two circumstances prompted Ernestine to become active in the 1960s. First, her daughter, Tina, began to row and then showed she had promise. Second, there was a move by some of the men's clubs to take over the PGRC boathouse on grounds that it was no longer sponsoring rowing programs. The result was that Ernestine became absolutely clear about her goal of making the PGRC a competitive rowing club, totally ignoring the undercurrent of discontent from members who were uncomfortable with the intensity of the kind of rowing she espoused.

As the Vichy competition drew near and the racers literally took over the club by living there, discontent among the other members began to fester. Ernie's women demanded the best shells, the most time. They weren't interested in the social aspirations of other club members. Their goal was to train, to race, and to win.

The dimensions of Ernie's personality dominated the scene. Just what kind of woman had she become?

Like all serious rowers, Ernie was committed and somewhat obsessive. An athlete since she was a child, she found magic in rowing, the alchemy of rower, shell, and water that a good stroke produces. Experienced rowers share the exhilaration that sending a shell through the water stimulates. It is a mental high that defies description; rowers recognize it when it happens, but then cannot describe exactly what happens. Instead, the euphoria of physical effort driving a shell remains a mystery, but once experienced, there is no going back. Rowers obsess about practice. They want to recapture that feeling of "send" again and again. It's a feeling that incorporates being weightless, free, powerful, and fast, yet being connected so that mind, body, water, rowing shell, and air create a unity made from perfect connections.

From almost her first row, Ernie experienced the exhilaration of sending a shell, and then, without the agony of indecision, devoted her life to making it happen for everyone she met, but most especially for women, who had been denied access to the sport for so long. Ernie's epiphany had come in the 1930s, way before the feminist movement of the 1960s led by such thinkers and doers as the late Betty Freidan, author of "The Feminine Mystique," and Gloria Steinem, her disciple. As the decade of the 1960s unfolded, Ernestine was not even a footnote in the well-documented feminist movement. In fact, she embraced the traditional social and behavioral values, except where rowing was concerned. And because she was regarded as a rowing feminist, she drew the dislike of the more traditional male rowers and more socially-oriented female rowers who were not interested in competition.

As Bernadette Andrews, one of the early PGRC rowers, put it when she joined at the age of fifteen, the PGRC during the 1950s had become a place of "cocktail and swim parties" and the reputation of the rowers was that they were "social creatures." The older women were not happy with Ernestine, she said. "They were there to have fun, not row."

By this time Ernie's vision, honed for almost twenty years, was in clear, sharp focus. Women should row. Her goal was so simple. Why should everyone else make it so complicated?

The men saw things in a different way.

Bill Stowe was the stroke of the Vesper gold medal-winning eight in the 1964 Olympics, a shell that represented a masculine club with the wealthiest and most experienced rowers. While he never really hated the idea of women's rowing, he said, "What I did not like was the women coming and demanding that

Ernestine, 1936   National Rowing Foundation

Ernest and Ernestine, chaperones for Tina's senior prom, 1963.
Bayer Family Files

Ernest and Ernestine, 1987   National Rowing Foundation

The Three Bayers: Ernest, Ernie, and Tina, early 1990s

Bayer Family files

Ernestine, 1932   Bayer Family files

everything be new without having earned it the way the men did."

Ernestine had earned her way many times over, and as she reactivated PGRC rowing she began to bring a certain rowing-oriented dignity to the club that changed its personality. "If it were not for Ernestine, girls' rowing would never have started because it was just not taken seriously," said Andrews.

Many years later, Carie Graves, a member of the 1984 gold medal-winning Olympic crew, compared herself to Ernie as a competitive person determined to row in spite of a culture that perceived her as doing "something different."

"Nothing was going to stop me from rowing," she said. "What I did and what Ernie did was because we were driven by really wanting to row, and loving it, and because we were in an environment where that was not usual. It was passion, and that's a good word for a woman…because we are women, we are very, very passionate."

Even before Vichy, Ernie had become a woman with a cause. She loved rowing, she loved competition, and she was not afraid to do what she had to do to accomplish her dream of equal opportunity for oarswomen in the world of men.

Those feelings intensified after Vichy. Richard Kuhn, a rower who knew her when he was a teenager, said that even at an early age his impression was that she thought of "basically nothing else but rowing. She would do anything for me or for anyone else, but her focus has always been on rowing or pushing people to make rowing happen. She never quits."

Both her looks and her energy augmented her determination. Small of stature, by today's standards for female rowers, she was blessed with clear skin and high cheekbones. Her personality was very direct; she had no patience with people who said they "couldn't." She did not know the meaning of the word "no." Her energy was inexhaustible.

"One of a kind," said Barbara Howe, who in 1966 was co-captain of one of Ernie's crews, and who rowed in the Vichy eight as Barbara DePena. "Ernie could alienate by her forcefulness. Some people can do okay under forceful people and some cannot. When I was co-captain, if you did not see things the way she saw them, well, you were just not on the train anymore. It was so interesting, and it translated into the lesson of life on how to get things done by working through a vision.

"As for her energy, you can't manufacture it and you can't define it. It's innate. She was meticulous, She could see things through. She worked on all details to make sure things didn't fall apart. In any other field she would have been a CEO. And if Plan A didn't work, she always had a Plan B. That's a really important lesson in life."

Despite her activity, Ernie never saw herself as a "women's libber."

"She was already liberated because of her love of rowing," said Mary Colgan, wife of a rower and close observer of the scene. "Ernie was really the Gloria Steinem of rowing. She tramped on a lot of toes, but that's what you had to do."

Bill Miller, a US National Team rower from 1969 to 1975, a master coach, and a historian of modern rowing, said that the significance of her activism was that when Title IX became law in 1973, mandating equal opportunities for college women in sports, Ernestine Bayer had laid the foundation for rowing to become a major women's sport at colleges and universities throughout the country.

Abby Peck, women's rowing coach at Wellesley and a member of the US Olympic women's crews in 1984 and 1988, described most succinctly Ernie's aggressive style in promoting women's rowing. "I got to know Ernie as her doubles partner in several races," she said. "She started women rowing and a lot of people didn't like her style. But you don't make waves without wetting people's pants."

CHAPTER 11:
TINA—RISE AND FALL
OF A ROWING CAREER

Tina competes in Klagenfurt, Austria, 1969
Bayer Family files

IN MANY RESPECTS, TINA BAYER'S ROWING CAREER BETWEEN the 1967 Vichy world competition and the Bayer family's move to New Hampshire in 1972 dominated the family's life. During these years, Ernie remained active as manager and captain of the PGRC and its chief cheerleader. Ernest Bayer was the strong, silent partner in the family, quietly giving his wife and daughter support as they weathered several crises in their respective rowing careers. He remained active in the male rowing community, commanding sufficient respect to be above the controversy Ernie still continued to generate.

The competitive focus, however, was on Tina, who knew she was right at the top of the dozen or so competitive women rowers in the country by virtue of her experience in the seven seat of the PGRC's eight, as well as in double sculls. Somewhat to her surprise, however, she discovered she was just as strong, possibly even stronger, in the single, and the nature of the shell proved to be an exact fit for her personality.

By 1967, the year of Vichy, Tina was twenty-two years old. Not surprisingly, she had inherited many of her mother's personality traits. She had a serious focus on rowing, she was fiercely competitive, and she was impatient with anyone who blocked her progress in the sport, whether they were other rowers or coaches.

The first big event for the PGRC rowers in 1968 was the Women's Nationals, to be held in Philadelphia for the first time. The first two had been on the West Coast. Tina and Margie Pollock, the coxswain of the women's eight that had competed at Vichy, were in charge of its organization. As hundreds of rowers since will attest, running a regatta, even a small one, is a highly complex operation, especially so the first time round. Rowing equipment must be lined up for visiting crews, as well as coach-boats, and adequate parking space. Referees and judges must be in place; timing and the course itself have to impeccable to insure fairness. Sleeping and eating arrangements, first aid stations, and getting the results out quickly are only a few of the other requirements. Then, there are always last minute hurdles such as illness, equipment breakdowns, and last, but hardly least, the weather.

The initial task Tina and Margie faced was putting together an equipment pool for the visiting rowers. Normally, for a national regatta, clubs at the venue supplied shells for the visiting crews. That was routine for men's crews, but it had never been done in Philadelphia for women's crews. At the most, they had previously borrowed one or two shells for a specific occasion. For the Women's Nationals, Tina needed thirty: six fours, six quads, six eights, six singles and six doubles. The idea that men's clubs would donate thirty regatta-quality shells for women was unthinkable in the Philadelphia boathouse culture.

"Putting together such a large equipment pool was a major headache," she said, "but we had to do it."

Fortunately, Tina had an ace in the hole: her father.

Ernest, the soft-spoken and highly-respected former Olympic rower, board member for the National Association of Amateur Oarsmen, coach, and referee, "the guy who would willingly do the detail work," as one admirer put it, began cashing in his chips. He personally visited all of the boathouses on Boathouse Row, asking for equipment.

"He was able to pull it off and we had our boats," said Tina.

Even so, there were problems.

For instance, one of the clubs lent two shells for the regatta, but with a huge condition attached: the boats were rigged for school boy championships that were to follow the women's competition and the coach would only lend the shells if the rigging were not changed.

Such a commitment is almost impossible to meet. Rowing essentially uses the leverage of the oar shaft and blade to send the shell forward. Rigging involves the adjustment of footstretchers, seat tracks, and outriggers to enable each rower to apply optimum leverage on the oar. The rigging process, then, somewhat resembles tailoring a suit or a dress for the best fit. Buying clothing off the rack that cannot be altered results in discomfort and misfits. So it is with racing shells. If they are not rigged to fit the body measurements of rowers, it is impossible for them to achieve their best performance potential.

One of the visiting coaches ignored the no re-rigging stricture and re-rigged the shell. When the donor club learned that he had done so, it pulled the rest of its shells from the regatta fleet.

"We had to go out and knock on doors all over again," said Tina. "And this was on the eve of the regatta."

For the PGRC, the first day of the competition was a nightmare of misfortunes involving accidents on the course and malfunctioning equipment.

The heavyweight quad race—four scullers, each with two oars in a shell with no coxswain—was a cliff-hanger. As the shell rounded St. Peter's Island, in first place with two lengths of open water, bow seat Evelyn Bergman's port oar hit an object that immediately dragged the blade down so that its shaft was almost perpendicular to the shell.

"The accident stopped the shell dead in the water. I was in the three seat and Penny Gibson was rowing in the two seat. I turned around and told Penny to grab the oar and yank. Penny leaned back and she and Evie yanked it out. By that time the Lake Merritt boat from California had passed us. We took a racing start and went after them, mowing them down just before the finish, passing them and winning the race. It was a quarter-mile dash," said Tina. Green Lake from Seattle was third.

But as in most accidents, once started the trouble escalates.

The quad rowed back to the launch area, upstream at the Canoe Club, for a quick exchange of crews from heavyweight to lightweight women.

As the exchange began, Tina left to row a doubles race with Nancy Farrell. Neither of her parents was around to consult. The other women took their seats in the quad only to find that the bow oarlock had been so damaged in the accident that the oar would not turn. The crew dropped out of the race and three of them rowed the shell back to Boathouse Row.

Tina was outraged."We won the eights and the heavyweight quad. We lost in the fours race, but we won in doubles and singles. We lost the trophy by one point. All that lightweight quad had to do was row down the course and we would have won the point trophy."

By 1969, increasingly sharp focus on her rowing career led to conflicts with the new coach, Gus Constant, who had left Vesper to join the PGRC. Gus brought with him a protégé, Ana Tamas-Raicu, a veteran international competitor from Romania. Ana had credentials. She was a ten-time Romanian single sculls champion from 1958 to 1967 and had won thirteen World Championship gold medals. Twenty-seven years old and a textile chemist, she had just defected to the United States.

Tina was convinced that Constant had a secret agenda in his subsequent make-up of the PGRC crews. That agenda, she believed, involved advancing the career of Ana Tamas-Raicu without regard to the combination of rowers that made sense for the team boats. She also found fault with Constant's coaching style and philosophy. The single became a natural outlet, because she could then focus on her own rowing.

The stakes were high for Tina in 1969, with the Fourth Annual Women's Regatta to be held on Seattle's Green Lake in June, a competition that would dictate the line-ups for the FISA European championships in Klagenfurt, Austria in September.

In the weeks preceding Seattle, she said, Constant decided that she and Nancy Farrell should row the double, a decision she found "an odd call, because both of us had always trained in the eight. Sure, we had rowed the double, but it was mostly hopping in at the last minute for a short row."

A couple of weeks before the regatta, Constant left for a weekend, leaving coaching duties to Ernest, her father, who had been running the coach-boat during practices. Ernest re-seated the eight with Nancy Farrell as stroke, Tina in the seven seat, and fill-in Penny Gibson in the six seat. He called for a time trial and the shell beat its previous record by twenty seconds.

"Gus came back on Monday and was faced with a crew saying that it wanted the three of us in the boat," Tina said. "Then there was all hell to pay."

Not only was the seating of the boat uncertain because of the weekend's lineup changes, there were financial issues. It became known that Constant was going to pay Ana's way to Seattle to compete in the single. Penny Gibson maintained that she had proved her value in the six seat, and if Constant paid Ana's way, then Constant should pay her's, too. Otherwise she could not afford the trip.

The lines of the dispute were drawn. Penny did not go to Seattle, and Constant put Ana in the six seat.

As soon as that happened, Tina said, communication within the boat fell apart because Ana, in the six seat, had trouble responding to the coxswain's instructions because of the language barrier. The result, she said, was the PGRC eight lost the nationals for the first time to the Seattle's Lake Washington Rowing Club, coming in second by about a length in the six-shell race.

"With no communication between the stern pair and the rest of the boat, we lost the Nationals," she said. "It was one of the most bitter races I have ever rowed. It was disgusting. We never expected it would happen. The cox did what she was supposed to do but we never got the information. The lack of communication killed us."

The Nationals were also a disaster for Tina in the singles competition. The initial heats resulted in six competitors qualifying for the final race with Tina, Ana, and Norma Jean Sands of the Lake Washington Rowing Club regarded as the strongest rowers.

In the hours before the race, the weather turned, serving up strong crosswinds on the course that whipped the waves high enough to break over the gunwales. Tina said that she knew that if Ana jumped her at the start, "I would never see her again, so my race plan was to stick with Ana. Period."

"That's what I did," she continued, "and for the first part it was almost a dead heat with Ana never ahead of me by more than three feet."

The wind, however, was blowing the frail boats off the un-buoyed course. (In fact, buoyed lanes were not to become features of US rowing courses for several more years. Many courses of that period had only start and finish line buoys and only sometimes buoys at the halfway mark.)

Tina said she was so focused on keeping up with Ana she did not know what was happening. As the race unfolded, Ana and Tina were in the lead, Norma Jean Sands and Sandy Garrett were battling for third and fourth, and far behind were the two stragglers.

In the motorboat at the rear, the officials were trying to warn the two lead boats that they were off course. Because of the distance between the lead boats and the stragglers, however, the warnings went unheeded, apparently unheard. Tina managed to row through Ana and then Ana abruptly stopped rowing.

"I shouted at her 'Are you okay?' and she just sat there over her oars. I thought, 'One of us has to win this race, this is stupid,' so I continued and finished first."

"I pulled into the dock and asked what happened to Ana. I didn't get an answer but by that time I had my boat out of the water just as the last boat crossed the finish line...and then I heard the announcement that I had been disqualified!"

Tina was absolutely stunned. She ran over to Gus Constant to ask why. Gus talked to the race referees. There followed a race committee meeting that she was not allowed to attend.

Then she was told the bad news. The race referee in the following coach-boat, she was told, had warned her three times that she was out of her lane and that she had ignored him. The penalty was disqualification.

"I never saw the referee," she said. "He was way back in the race. There was an enormous headwind in that part of the race. Waves were crashing over the riggers. The referee did not have a megaphone. Instead he was cupping his hands. There was not a chance in hell I could have heard him. I was very angry. I was cheated."

The upshot was that Ana finished third because of her stop and Norma Jean Sands, who came in second, won the national medal.

Later Tina learned that the race committee had asked Ana why she stopped in mid-race. Ana reportedly told the committee that she had to stop rowing or she would have rowed into Tina's shell. She claimed interference. Tina said Ana never spoke to her about the incident.

Several years later Tina received a letter of apology from the referee. "I have since learned more about the Rules of Racing and have concluded that I never should have disqualified you that day. I realize I cost you a national championship and you have my sincere apologies," he wrote.

Tina was not about to give up. She believed that, in spite of the penalty, she was the national women's champion and as such she was determined to compete in the late summer European championships in Klagenfurt, Austria. The problem was that officially Sands was the national champion and therefore would be selected to represent the US in the European competition. Sands had already expressed her determination to compete in Klagenfurt.

Tina prevailed. The then-rules allowed her to challenge Sands in the single and if she won she would represent the US at Klagenfurt. Sands declined the challenge, a move that paved the way for Tina to go to Austria as defending US women's singles champion. She would be the first US woman to compete in singles against an international field. Klagenfurt, however, was a disappointment. Tina rowed against a field of much more experienced European oarswomen, finishing tenth out of eleven.

"I did beat Yugoslavia but only because the Yugoslavian rower had a coughing fit in the middle of the race," she said.

After Klagenfurt, Tina's competitive rowing career was over, at least for the next several years.

"I had achieved something," she said. "It was a fight but after Klagenfurt and the horrible experience at the Nationals in both the eight and singles, I just burned out as far as competitive rowing was concerned."

Ana Tamas-Raicu went on to have a distinguished rowing career. She was the first woman to coach at Vesper Boat Club in the early 1970s. She also coached the Irish National Sculling Team at Munich in 1972, as well as the Canadian women's silver medal straight pair in the 1976 Olympics. She died of cancer on January 1, 1992.

CHAPTER 12:
MALE CHAUVINISM IN THE 1970s... AS PORTRAYED IN *THE OARSMAN* BY EMORY CLARK

Reprinted from English Magazine **Rowing**

WHILE ERNIE BROKE THROUGH THE MALE CHAUVINISM that was so apparent in Philadelphia rowing during the 1960s, those attitudes towards women rowers were to prevail through the early 1970s. By the end of the decade, thanks to Title IX and the 1976 Olympics, they had dissipated. By the 1984 Olympics, they were all but gone. Even though Ernie never considered herself a feminist in the usual sense of the word, her efforts in the 1960s were to have a profound impact in shaping a rowing environment that came of age during the 1980s, when women could finally share the sport with men. Not only could they share, they were enthusiastically welcomed.

Joe Sweeney, the Boathouse Row historian, put the matter of male chauvinism in perspective, observing that "in the 1930s and before the idea of women rowing was just something so far out of the mainstream that it was not even an issue. Women did not row. Period. They never had, they never would. They weren't built for such a grueling sport. Today, with so many women who have proved themselves in the sport, it is just surprising that at one time, we all thought that way. But we did. That's the way it was."

Since then, male attitudes towards women have undergone profound changes. The 1960s feminists mounted the initial assault on traditional male behavior, demanding equal treatment in all aspects of life. Their ideas and actions provoked anger, discomfort, wonder, and finally grudging acceptance from the male population.

A good example of how the gender issue began to play out in the rowing community is seen in the writing of Emory Clark, a contributor to *The Oarsman*, the official publication of the National Association of Amateur Oarsmen. Clark had ample credentials. A 1960 graduate of Yale University, he was an oarsman on the 1964 Olympic Gold Medal eight. At first he made fun of the early women rowers, then he came to accept them. By the end of the 1970s decade, he was a cheerleader.

In a September 1970 article with the headline "A Woman's View of St. Catherines" which then would have come under the label of "humor," Clark fashioned a letter from "Christina" to "Mary" about the just-completed World Championships at St. Catherines, Ontario, Canada. Excerpts follow:

> We had a grand time with the weather, just perfect, so I got to wear my new grey outfit on Saturday and my yellow pant-suit for the finals...But never mind the wardrobe, Mary, I've found the man for you. I mean, you've simply got to come to the next one of these things. He's not very tall, but he has immensely

powerful shoulders, long black sideburns, romantic eyes, and he's Argentine. I never quite got his name, but he won the single sculls, which probably doesn't matter much to you...

The most fun was Sunday before the finals when they got me into the enclosure around the docks and the boat sheds—I had to climb a wicked wire fence because they had guards all around to keep people like me out, and I almost ruined my suit, but it was worth it—besides dozens of handsome men with next to nothing on, they had a food stand with free ice cream. Well, my dear, it was as if St. Peter had let me through the Gates before my time ...

Well, I better stop rambling, Mary. I'm getting worse than Emory with this rowing business, but I must tell you about some of the people first, because just everybody comes to these regattas—it's like a giant fraternity party with all the old grads back. There's Harry Parker, the Harvard coach, looking wiser than it is possible for anyone to be and inscrutable as the Sphinx....and, of course, Thomi Keller, a charming dignified perfectionist who heads the International Rowing Federation and, Emory says, puts the competitors first, unlike so many other old fogey sports officials. ... He's Swiss and always speaks to you (or drinks with you) in your own language no matter what country you're from. ...

In a more serious article in May 1972, entitled "Rowing and the Constitution or Can a Girl Find Equality on the River," Clark confesses that he is a male chauvinist and then concedes, "Eight girls in a boat are a stimulating sight. The sport is healthy and fun for them and if they're going to bet shirts, no doubt they will handle the payoff discreetly. ..." He continues:

Did not Congress just approve another Constitutional amendment giving women absolute equality? What is that supposed to mean if not that some dimpled damsel can take my seat if she can make the boat go

faster...I suppose if I were not a male chauvinist I
would cant some such litany as 'I don't care who rows
in front of me as long as she moves the boat.' Congress
says she is equal and I voted, didn't I? But is she going
to do five sets of 20 squat jumps with a 35-lb weight
clasped to her bosom? Is she going to take it in the
right spirit when I point out with the proper profane
emphasis that her blade is not buried in the middle
of the stroke? Will she insist on a separate shower so
I'll have no way of positively assuring whether she has
lost the requisite amount of weight?

Clark wrote another series of three articles entitled "The
Bride's Revenge" about a just married woman named Harriet who
married a rower named Harry, then decided to row herself. She
became quite proficient and then devoted more time to rowing
than to her husband and became physically stronger than him in
the process.

Harry, the rower, complains to his mother that he thought he
had married someone "to build a home around, to have children
with, to come home to, to love ..."

Mother, you remember how single-minded I was when
I was rowing, how passionate. ... Harriet's the same
way. If the President declared war on Russia, her first
thought would be whether war would make her miss
a workout and who she could get to babysit if my
reserve unit were called up. ...I've got real trouble, not
the least of which is how am I going to make it to little
Harriet's Parent-Teacher Conference next Friday when
I'm supposed to be at a sales meeting in Omaha and
Harriet says she'll be loading boats at the Boat Club all
day...

Clark reports that Harriet subsequently decided to row in the
1976 Olympics which meant she would be seeing another Harry,
in this case Harry Parker, the well-known Harvard coach. He asks
his mother:

What do we know about this Harry? Nothing! Those girls will do anything to make the boat. It's indecent. It's obscene. They should have women coaches. Why should a happily married, perfectly contented mother of two put herself in the hands of some other Harry?

"Harry," says his mother, "may I remind you this is 1976. Husbands don't forbid anymore. Anyway, Harriet has already left."

I know. That's what hurts. She said she had to catch a ride and would I be a dear and pick up my shirts at the laundry and to look in Wednesday's paper for the specials at the A&P and she left me a phone number. ...

In a more serious article, "Oarswomen: Separate but Not Yet Equal," Clark comments:

If the girls want to paddle around and enjoy themselves, that is fine, as long as they do not get in the way. If they do well, that's fine. But there is nothing quite like the men's heavyweight eight churning off the line at a 48. Right? I'm afraid so. Deep-seated prejudices will not wash out overnight. As I have stated, mine are intact.

By the end of the decade, however, Clark had begun to lose those prejudices. Following the 1976 Olympics, he wrote:

Aside from the smile on US boxer Sugar Ray Leonard's face when he heard the decision awarding him a gold medal, the most beautiful sight I saw at the games was Joan Lind. With her medal around her neck, being greeted and congratulated outside the stands at the Olympic Basin, she made one proud to be an American...

Certainly going by the two criteria by which all Olympians are judged (the winning and the taking part), Joan, America's first woman to win a silver medal in rowing, was the US rowing world's brightest moment.

Finally, in 1979, he wrote a glowing article as an advance to the Women's National Regatta to begin on June 14 in Detroit. "The activity is feverish," he reported. "...eighty-seven committees are working pell-mell for their June deadline and if the organizers are as ready as the oarswomen are fit, it promises to be the finest women's regatta ever held in North America."

CHAPTER 13:
MOVE TO
NEW HAMPSHIRE

A FTER KLAGENFURT, TINA DECIDED SHE HAD TO GET ON with her career. She had accepted a full-time job in data processing at the John Hancock Insurance Company in Boston and was commuting to Boston from Rye, New Hampshire, where the Bayers had rented a house. For a short time, Ernie also took a job at John Hancock as a legal secretary and made the commute with her daughter. Ernest Bayer had retired in 1969 after forty-six years with the First Pennsylvania Banking and Trust Company where he was vice president.

At the PGRC, the undercurrent of unrest intensified during the late 1960s. Despite a focus on national and international racing, there was still an element that preferred a more relaxed approach to the sport and to the administration of the club. Members of that group had simply grown tired of Ernie's pushiness.

In marked contrast to the much quieter 1950s, the years between 1965 and 1975 were ones of protest and discontent in many elements of American society. While the changing social and cultural environment may not have had a direct effect on the PGRC, nevertheless the events of that period led to profound changes in most institutions.

During the 1950s, young men and women had been able to look forward to lives with traditional boundaries. Americans had just burst out of urban environments, flocking to open spaces and then building suburbias, their behavior governed by the calming and respected administration of President Eisenhower. Traditional moral values continued to hold sway. There was limited opportunity for sex before marriage because of fears of pregnancy, the US was not at war, and Catholic and Protestant churches were still social and moral arbiters. In this gauzy environment, young people graduated from high school or college, they found jobs, they married, they had children, and they acquired houses, lawns, dogs, station wagons.

That secure and somewhat staid way of life came to an abrupt end in the 1960s. The youthful and vibrant John F. Kennedy introduced the decade upon his election in November 1960. Before his assassination, he had unwittingly made the moves that led to the Vietnam War. Rosa Parks, a black woman, struck the small spark that would become the roaring fire of the Civil Rights movement of the 1960s, which contributed to a gathering storm of change that increased in intensity as the decade unfolded. By 1965, incidents of violence and nonviolence had begun to saturate the social fabric, begetting dramatic and charismatic leaders, black and white, who became household names. College students marched against the Vietnam War and forcefully occupied campus buildings. President Lyndon Johnson saw his reputation as a statesman descend into tatters. On April 4, 1968, the Rev. Martin Luther King Jr., the charismatic civil rights leader, was assassinated. Two months later, on June 4, 1968, Robert F. Kennedy, then the Attorney General and a frontrunner for the Democratic nomination, was assassinated. "Clean Gene" McCarthy, a distinctly nontraditional candidate, made a serious bid for the US presidency, running on a peace platform. Four students were killed at Kent State University in Ohio when the National Guard opened fire during a war protest on May 4, 1970, provoking thousands of others to walk off their campuses.

In the meantime, the late Betty Freidan wrote "The Feminine Mystique," a book that changed the thinking of millions of young women who vowed to claim their place in the sun. Her disciple, Gloria Steinem, led them to the barricades of resistance. The birth control pill became a reality, freeing women from the fear of pregnancies that might result from exciting, but casual, relationships. Recreational drugs, especially marijuana, became popular among the young. So did miniskirts and the bra-less look.

Ernie, who had been regarded as such a rebel because she stood up to the male rowing community, was fifty-eight years old in 1967 when the various protest and liberation movements began to grip the nation and transform society. Her values, however, outside of rowing, remained traditional.

"I am not a feminist," she once declared when asked about her feelings about the various movements upsetting society. Instead, she said, men were instrumental in opening the sport of rowing for women. She did not want to challenge men, in the way of the feminists. Instead, she wanted to bring men into her fold, helping them see the error of their ways in regard to women's rowing. For the most part, she admired men and was quick to say that without the support of certain key men—her husband, Ted Nash, John Quinn, and a few others—the PGRC would not have succeeded.

She also did not understand the lack of commitment to the sport that she perceived among some of the younger women who had joined the club in the 1960s. For her, serious rowing by both men and women required discipline and acceptance of rules. Yes, she was a woman who could fight with every skill she had for the right of women to row. But she was still a woman, and she still held traditional values when it came to issues of rules, dress, behavior, language, and sexual conduct.

In the late 1960s, the schism within the PGRC grew wider and deeper. Tina attributed it to a difference in goals. For instance, she said, as the nationals approached in 1969, she and Nancy Farrell openly expressed their wish to win the double

123

at the nationals so they could qualify to race in the European championships in Klagenfurt, Austria, later that year. The night before the finals for the nationals, she said, the other crew members asked that they scratch the double because they were afraid that the physical effort for the doubles race would sap their performance in the eight.

Tina said she then asked whether, if the eight did win, the crew would race in Klagenfurt. The answer, she said, was no, so she and Nancy stuck to their plan.

She called it an example of vacillation in the club. The competitive members said they wanted to be at the top, but then hesitated to make the sacrifices that would put them there.

The lack of consensus on competitive goals between the Bayers and other members of the club became so serious that even in 2006, nearly forty years later, people who are now the older members politely decline to speak specifically about the situation that prevailed. They do not want to go back to re-visit its particulars or to criticize a woman in her nineties who, most will now acknowledge, did so much to advance women's rowing.

More specifically, the discontent revolved around Ernie's style of management, and Tina's competitive intensity. Mother and daughter both knew what they wanted; both knew where they wanted the club to go.

One club member at the time said that the nation's political climate had nothing to do with internal dynamics of the club and that "we were unaffected." Yet the events at the PGRC took place against a backdrop of national turmoil and change. Another said she thought Ernie wanted to be the John Kelly Jr. of the PGRC. For many years, in an earlier, quieter time, Kelly had been the driving force at Vesper. Whatever he said, or thought, was accepted without question. Ernie believed herself to be the same kind of driving force. She had been in the trenches, she had taken the crew to Vichy, she had paid her dues, and she expected—indeed demanded—to be The Word at the PGRC. Still another member said, "She stepped over the edge with too many people."

A shift in the background of some club members since the 1930s may also have contributed to the problems. During the 1960s, women who had recently graduated from college began to join. They were much more independent, with good jobs and salaries much higher than those commanded by the earlier "office girl" rowers. They were active in the women's movement, in civil rights and political actions. Some just wouldn't "buy in" to Ernie Bayer's persona and style. Furthermore, there was a terrific age difference. Ernie was in her fifties; these newer members were much younger, part of the generation of "flower children" who rebelled against the establishment and whose clarion call was "Never trust anyone over thirty."

There were other members who were perhaps not so militant, but they were sick and tired of the spotlight on Ernie. She received all of the credit, or so they thought. This group believed themselves to be just as active, but found they were not receiving the recognition they thought they deserved. And to make matters worse, knowingly or unknowingly Ernie herself did not always acknowledge their merits in spite of their loyalty, work, and financial contributions.

Finally, there were some specific issues that created division. One concerned the upkeep of the boathouse building which the club occasionally rented to outside groups for parties. Who would make the building ready for the party? Who would clean up the premises after the party? Those questions inevitably led to discord between the Bayers and some of the members.

The upshot was that there was a mutiny of sorts. Rowers began to leave the club. One group even tried to form its own club. The time had simply come, as it does in so many organizations, for the person with the original vision to step out of the way.

"And yet," as one member of that era put it, "Ernie was the one who made the club what it was. She put us on the map. She was the driving force, she broke the ice…but she was also in everybody's face and some people just didn't like it, even though she really was the one who deserved the credit for starting it all."

Penny Gibson Henwood, who had rowed at Vichy, said the situation created distress for her and for other early members. "We won a lot of medals but she was losing the club," she observed.

As discontent festered within the club, Tina's life had become much more complicated. She had been working in center city Philadelphia for the Insurance Company of North America, which had decided to move to Cherry Hill, NJ. That move would mean a two-hour commute so she began to explore other opportunities, including those in New England.

"I found I loved New England," she said, and in 1971 she accepted a job at the John Hancock company. She was then twenty-six years old. After she had established herself, her mother and father left Philadelphia to join her. The family first lived in Rye, New Hampshire.

Ernie did not know it at the time, but the move to New Hampshire meant that she would restart her rowing career, this time in a completely different direction. She would also find that she would develop a culture that was considerably more forgiving than the one she had left in Philadelphia.

PART II:
NEW HAMPSHIRE

JEANNE FRIEDMAN GREW UP IN PHILADELPHIA AND CAME TO know Ernie during her college years when she started rowing at the PGRC. She subsequently had a distinguished career that included national championships in both singles and sweep shells. She became head rowing coach at Mount Holyoke College in Massachusetts in 1992 and has since maintained the close friendship she had developed with Ernie.

Summing up her mentor's contributions to rowing, she said, "Ernie not only made it possible for young women to row, she also laid the groundwork for older women to row, beginning in Philadelphia and continuing with the Alden Ocean Shell Association in New Hampshire.

"She proved three things during her life: First, women can row; second, women can row fast; and third, women can row no matter how old they are. In her later years, she could even say 'Look at me, I'm ninety, and I'm still rowing.'"

Ernestine Bayer not only broke the mold of the male rowing culture because she opened the sport for women; she also broke another mold in New England, where she became a major influence in developing an entirely different rowing culture: recreational rowing for older people and for children.

She was not alone. The breakthrough really came in the early 1970s when the late Arthur E. Martin designed a curious craft called the Alden Ocean Shell and then moved his fledgling company to Kittery Point, Maine, a seacoast hamlet separated from New Hampshire only by the Piscataqua River. His craft was a sixteen-foot stubby looking shell that "anybody could row anywhere" a boast that appeared in an early company promotion. Shortly after her move to New Hampshire, Ernie bought one of the first shells he had manufactured and immediately saw that this shell could attract an enormous number of people to rowing without the need of boathouses and extensive coaching.

Until then, most rowers were boathouse-focused and spoke boathouse language that revolved around racing, equipment, coaches, physical conditioning, and money. The result was a culture with principal eastern centers in Philadelphia, Boston, New Haven, and Princeton. With the discovery of the Alden, Ernie set about to create an entirely different culture based primarily on rowing in singles as opposed to team boats; car-top transportation of equipment as opposed to trailers; sawhorse storage of shells or just leaving them turned over like rowboats, instead of boathouses and racks; and relaxed fellowship among active but not necessarily athletic people, who just enjoyed rowing for the sake of rowing and competition so long as it was not too serious.

Rowing is a wet sport -- Even at Lake Winnipesaukee, NH
Lew Cuyler

CHAPTER 14:
<u>ARTHUR MARTIN</u>

Arthur Martin   Marjorie Burgard Files

THE STORY OF THE ALDEN OCEAN SHELL ASSOCIATION BEGINS with the late Arthur Martin. In 1990, Arthur wrote his autobiography, entitled "Life in the Slow Lane," telling the story of how the Alden had changed his own life and in the process, through Ernestine Bayer, the rowing culture.

The jacket cover of his book, slightly edited, provides the following synopsis.

> *His boyhood on the Maine coast, intimately dependent upon all kinds of small boats for the necessities of life as well as its pleasures, nurtured a lifelong love as well as a successful professional career in boat design. Kent School (a private college preparatory school in Connecticut)*

*provided him the opportunity to row in an eight-oared
shell, as well as a single wherry, and generated a clash of
ideas and personalities with Father Sill (headmaster and
crew coach) and others in authority.*

*At Webb Institute of Naval Architecture, Martin received
his necessary technical education and endured some
tense but amusing confrontations with Admiral Rock, the
authoritarian man in charge…the book invites readers
to join in a slower, more thoughtful lifestyle, with the
appreciation of God and nature, and the healthy body
which many abuse by cigarettes, drugs, alcohol, rich foods
and lack of exercise.*

*The Alden Ocean Shell, originally conceived as a home
hobby project, brought fame to the boat, the designer, and
the little town of Kittery Point, Maine, which became the
company headquarters. …*

The Alden shell heralded the use of fiberglass as the prime
material in making rowing shells. Up until the late 1960s, rowing
shells were made of wood, principally cedar and mahogany,
by men with the same skills that were used for fine furniture
making. The shells were beautiful pieces of work, visually
tremendously appealing. The foremost American shell-maker
of the 1950s and 1960s was George W. Pocock of Seattle,
whose company provided most of the shells for the college
and university crews. Pocock's name and skills were revered
throughout the rowing world.

Arthur Martin had grown up in a world of wooden boats
and he continued that love during the first part of his adult
life in Cohasset, Massachusetts, a commuter and sailing village
just south of Boston, where he worked with friends—two of
them boat designers—designing, building, and testing small
boats, mostly as a hobby. However, he had become increasingly
unhappy with his business career, mostly spent in sales for larger
companies.

In 1970, he wrote, "I accepted a job with the John Alden Company in Boston and left the world of big business forever." The highly-respected Alden company was New England's major yacht builder. Curiously, Arthur's job was not in boat design— the company already had the top boat designers in its employ— it was in brokerage and marine insurance. Those duties did not matter, he wrote. Instead, "it was great to be back in the boat business and apply myself to the task of all that had taken place in the twenty-three years I had been away from it."

More importantly, the environment of Arthur's new job encouraged him to continue his hobby of designing small boats. As he began working with the Alden company, his spare time project was the design of a kayak. And it was that design that eventually emerged as a fiberglass rowing shell, unlike any that ever been made.

Arthur described his thinking behind his then-unnamed "little rowing shell" and he wondered whether the hidebound rowing community would or would not accept such a distinctively different craft.

Up until the late 1960s, he wrote, "The sculling boats, in which each rower handles two oars, or sculls, approximately nine-feet-nine inches long, were the single, the double, the quad, and the almost extinct octopede. The dimensions, shapes, and construction of all of these boats had evolved over the years in an effort to get the maximum speed from their human propulsion systems over a short course on perfectly smooth water.

"Use of all of these boats was limited almost entirely to a few Ivy League schools and colleges, and exclusive clubs, some of which to this day do not welcome the fair sex. Americans seemed to retain a certain snobbishness about rowing, possibly derived from their former rulers in England. Although exercise was beginning to be recognized as a significant factor in health, the one form now widely acclaimed as the best of all, rowing with a sliding seat, seemed to be a secret, jealously guarded by its elitist practitioners."

Arthur had had enough experience in the boathouse culture to realize its focus on the single shell, a 26–28 foot magnificent piece of wood furniture designed to go fast. He also knew that coaching had improved sufficiently that boathouses were no longer using the wider wooden trainer shells to teach single shell rowing. Instead, the clubs were saving money on equipment by skipping the training shell process, and starting novice rowers in the racing shells.

He wanted to design a rowing shell everyone could use. "The question was," he wrote, "would any of the sliding-seat rowing fraternity have any use for a boat which was not like a racing shell at all, except that it was rowed with a sliding seat?"

He turned his thoughts to the non-boathouse world of rowing. That other world, he wrote "included all of the people who, like myself, had grown up with a love of rowing in peapods, dories, Whitehalls, Adirondack guide boats, Saint Lawrence skiffs, and other seaworthy, stable, and versatile boats with fixed seats. These people were inclined to view with scorn the snobby landlubbers who required perfectly flat, protected water to pursue their narrow, single-purpose sport. On the other hand, hardly anyone from the racing world had any use for the slow, heavy, fixed-seat boats of the other world, or their plodding, fishing, picnicking, bird-watching adherents.

"Would the people of both worlds look with scorn on our little boats, which really were not a part of either one?" he asked. Then he answered himself with the notion that indeed the racing shell people might well accept his ideas because the boat he hoped to create would enable them to do many things that they could not do in a racing shell.

Former competitive rowers, he believed, now older, grown up, busy with career and family, "might relish the opportunity of rowing wherever water, rough or smooth, was within driving distance."

"Still others," he continued, might be enticed by durability, stowability, or the safety of stability in cold water. ..."

He almost lost his nerve when he figured out the investment needed to bring it to market. As it turned out, the president of the company, Neil Tillotson, had a soft spot for entrepreneurial boat-builders. The second partner in the company, Everett Pearson, had just started a spin-off company making smaller sailboats out of fiberglass.

These two developments—Tillotson's enthusiasm for entrepreneurial boat-building and Pearson's fiberglass sailboat enterprise, which could also handle the manufacture of another kind of small fiberglass boat—made it clear to Arthur that if he wanted to go through with his idea of producing a new kind of rowing shell, the opportunity to do so was at hand.

He explained his idea to Neil Tillotson and won his blessing. Not only that, but Tillotson "kindly agreed to let us use Mr. Alden's prestigious name for the new boats. I had met John Alden, whom I admired greatly, but he had died long before I designed the Alden Ocean Shell. As Neil Tillotson pointed out, he owned the Alden name and it was due to the generosity of this fine gentleman that we were able to introduce our unique boats under such a famous name."

There was a condition, however. Tillotson said that if Arthur decided to develop his idea, he would have to pay for the molds and tooling needed to produce the boat, and that he would also have to guarantee the sale of twenty of his new boats during its first year.

"This confronted me with a difficult decision," Arthur wrote. "My carefully-hoarded savings would be gone forever, in exchange for some worthless tooling if the project failed.

I figured I could sell one boat to my generous mother and a couple more to devil-may-care friends, but then I would be stuck with seventeen white elephants."

That didn't happen. The Alden Ocean Shell was introduced at the Boston Boat Show in 1971. Arthur had worked day and night, not only in its production but also its marketing. He also had some major breaks in favorable press coverage of the new craft. Best of all, Harry Parker, then a young rowing coach at Harvard University, and already a man whose name and career commanded great respect in the rowing community, became interested in the Alden. It was Parker, along with Ernestine Bayer, who advised Arthur that it needed full-size racing oars and longer riggers to improve its performance. So highly respected was Parker that other coaches took notice and, by Arthur's account, "began to recommend our boats for older people, recreational rowers, and even competing oarsmen for practice in the off-season, when water is cold or the usual rowing situation is not available."

By the end of 1972, the first year of production, he had sold 165 shells, way over the twenty he had promised he would sell when he made the agreement with Neil Tillotson. He decided to leave the Alden company so he could devote himself full-time to his new enterprise. He also moved from Cohasset to Kittery Point, Maine, where living was cheaper and he would be nearer to his beloved Isles of Shoals, a reef seven miles out to sea, and a favorite spot for rowing when he first fell in love with boats as a boy.

By coincidence, 1971 was the year the Bayers moved to New Hampshire.

CHAPTER 15:

<u>THE AOSA</u>

Ernestine Bayer and Marjorie Martin Burgard share a row in a double.
Photo probably taken in 1980s.   Bayer Family files

ERNIE AND HER FAMILY MOVED TO RYE, NEW HAMPSHIRE
in November 1971. The move made sense in their
personal lives. Tina, her commute now manageable,
continued to work at John Hancock, and Ernest found
a part-time bookkeeping job. Ernie and Tina, however, were
not particularly satisfied with their rented house, nor were they
happy with the lack of rowing opportunities.

Ernie, not knowing about the rivers in the state, searched
for a place to row and to store the racing singles she and Tina
owned. Within a few months she thought she was successful,
but the place was not right. The Bayers' new "boathouse" was a
marina in Hampton, a nearby village on New Hampshire's coast,
a popular seaside resort destination. Ernestine was thrilled when
the marina owners, who knew nothing about racing shells, gave
her permission to store the shells in a repair shop. What she did

not know, however, was that storage meant putting each shell into two slings, one in the bow and one in the stern, and then hoisting them sixty feet off the floor and out of the way. The arrangement was cumbersome for two women used to racking up boats in a boathouse with water and a low dock only a few boat-lengths away.

Neither had they expected the offshore boat traffic that threatened their fragile wooden rowing singles. The traffic included large sailboats that could not maneuver very well, small sailboats that darted back and forth, water skiers, and motorboats that created excessive wake. The plethora of lobster pot buoys posed a constant threat to the thin hulls of their shells. The wind and the waves created still more risks for them. After lifetimes on the placid waters of the Schuylkill River, where rowing patterns were well established and motorboat behavior was predictable, rowing in the Hampton Bay was intolerable.

Ernest was not rowing, but day after day during their first summer in New Hampshire he had to listen to the complaints of his wife and daughter. Late in the season, Ernie spotted an ad for a rental house at nearby Kittery Point, Maine, on the Spruce Creek, a quiet waterway. At about the same time, Ernest mentioned that he had heard "about this guy from Kittery Point who was making a different kind of rowing shell that could be used in the ocean." That clinched the decision. Further inquiry led to the identification of Arthur Martin, followed in quick order by a phone call and an invitation to try out his shell.

The Bayers moved into their Kittery Point property in November 1972, just as the rowing season ended. They loved their new house. Even better, its location was within a three mile rowable distance from Arthur and Marjorie Martin who lived on Chauncey Creek.

What a happy mix of circumstances for Ernie Bayer! Her love of rowing was unabated, but she was in New Hampshire, where she could not row in her accustomed manner. And here was a man—indeed, almost a next door neighbor—who had made a boat that was tough and could be rowed. Moreover, he was interested in racing.

The connection was electric.

Ernie was then sixty-three. Marjorie Burgard, Arthur Martin's widow who has since remarried, recalled that she was then in her forties, that she had always loved to row, and that this unlikely white-haired woman, along with her husband, had abruptly appeared in their driveway.

"I had no idea who she was, but we quickly discovered we both loved to row," she said. "I had never before talked to someone who loved to row as much as I did."

The upshot was that Ernie and Arthur ended up rowing a double together that afternoon. She immediately liked Arthur's unconventional but eminently rowable shell, and she bought a double with the hope that she could re-kindle Ernest's interest in rowing because they could use the shell together. She was unaware of the fact that in making the purchase, she had just entered a dramatic new phase in her life in which she would have just as much influence on rowing as she had during the thirty-five years she had spent rowing in Philadelphia.

So excited was Ernestine about her discovery of a shell that she could row in coastal waters that with characteristic enthusiasm she proposed to Arthur that he should create an association of Alden owners who could race against each other and stage various other events.

"Arthur, this is a great boat. It is just right for all kinds of rowers. I love it. It's a real grassroots boat and you could have some fun with it. You could have an association. It would be great," she told him.

She said Arthur was polite but she could tell he really didn't share her enthusiasm. He said he did not did not want to deal with the liability issues that might arise with an association. He also feared that that open-water racing might mean that to be fair different kinds of boats would have to be rated for hull drag information, as was required for sailboat racing.

"No, no," said Ernie in one of those earlier conversations. "You could just have one-class racing. Only Aldens would race. The liability situation could be resolved if the association joined the US Rowing Association as a club and thus became eligible for its liability insurance as a club member." She offered to run the association.

Arthur had just begun his second season manufacturing shells and he was still feeling his way. He wasn't so sure he was enthusiastic about Ernie's idea. Despite what she said, there could be liability issues. Administration would be another problem. And yet, he had always loved rowing to the Isles of Shoals, a collection of small rocky islands about seven miles off the coast. Why not a race?

"It dawned on me that a race could not be anywhere else but the Isles of Shoals. It was certainly appropriate that the first race of Alden Ocean Shells should be on the open ocean. Then there was the continuity of the strongest thread of my early life, which had great appeal for me. The thought of a group of our little boats rowing out to the magic islands which played such a big part in my life gave me a great feeling of nostalgia..." he wrote.

Ernie's ideas were intriguing. In fact, she was becoming persuasive. Expressing his thoughts in his book, he wrote, "With increasing numbers of Alden rowers, it was inevitable that some of them would want to see how fast they could go in relation to others. A race between an Alden and a dory wouldn't make much sense...on the other hand, it would be equally foolish to have a race between an Alden and a racing shell. But a race where all of the rowers were in identical boats would be just as fair and exciting as a race between the obviously faster racing sculls.

In 1972 he organized the first Isles of Shoals race. Much to his disappointment, thick fog made it impossible and dangerous to row the seven miles to the Isles. The race was held, but on a shorter course closer to shore.

Following the race, Arthur invited everyone to his house for lunch, where he offered a drink that he called Cransauvod, made of one quarter vodka, one quarter sauterne, and one half cranberry juice. The effects of the drink made everyone enthusiastic about the Isles of Shoals race, even though weather had prevented the initial attempt to row to the Shoals.

Ernie, who had not rowed in that first race, nevertheless saw an opening and she pounced. Again, with her characteristic enthusiasm, she suggested that Alden owners should form an association to encourage further races, expressing the idea that she had already proposed to Arthur. She volunteered to run the association. She did not envision a boathouse, but she did envision an association of owners who could share experiences and organize events.

The assemblage liked the idea, but as so often happens at those occasions, the notion might have flared and then died, because of the details and commitment it entailed. Putting on such a race, especially for seven miles in the open ocean, requires a lot of organization, not to mention safety measures.

Arthur wrote, "The problem appeared to be beyond the capability or willingness of the assembled company. Except for Ernestine Bayer."

However, in the end, he could not hold out against her persuasiveness and enthusiasm. And he liked the idea of rowing to his beloved Isles of Shoals.

Ernie set about organizing what came to be known as the Alden Ocean Shell Association. One of the first things she did was to put together a packet of information that Arthur could distribute to buyers. It told them about the association and how they could join. Ernie was the self-appointed secretary and treasurer of the association for the next sixteen years, finally resigning her duties in 1988. By then she had recruited an estimated 700–800 members to the organization for various periods of time. The early files of the AOSA contain hundreds of personal letters she wrote to new and prospective members, infecting the entire organization with her enthusiasm.

As one of her first initiatives for the fledgling AOSA, she embarked on the almost unthinkable notion to have the Head of the Charles organization in Cambridge accept Alden rowers as competitors. The Head of the Charles, then and now, is the largest and most prestigious non-college rowing regatta in the United States. Each fall it attracts the best national and international rowers to engage in a challenging three-mile head race along the twisting Charles River course. Seasoned rowers regard the course as the world's most competitive racing venue because its many bends force rowers, especially scullers who face backwards, to navigate as well as to row. The regatta had never been opened to the non-racing variety of rowing shell.

Darcy McMahon of Boston, one of the early organizers of the Head of the Charles, knew Ernie by reputation. He said that in the first year the Head of the Charles was run, 1965, there were no separate events for women.

"Without any pre-announcement, two fours from the PGRC showed up. Ernie was in one of them—she was sixty-one years old at the time—and her daughter, Tina, was in the second. We didn't know what to do, so on the spot we decided that we would let them row an 'exhibition' race."

In 1972, McMahon received a letter from Ernie, saying that

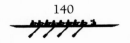

the Alden Ocean Shell Association planned to enter shells in the Head of the Charles race. "The Aldens were a problem for us," he said. "It wasn't that we didn't like Aldens, but they were a new kind of shell, we didn't know much about them, and they certainly were not racing shells. They just didn't fit what we were doing."

In addition, he said, the rowing shell business is competitive, and the regatta's board members believed that if they ran a race exclusively for Aldens, it would set a bad precedent for favoritism of a particular manufacturer.

Ernie, now joined by Tina, agreed, and, as usual, both were persistent. They said the Alden race could be separate from the Charles organization. They accepted, indeed promoted, the idea for a separate category for open water shells other than Alden. The AOSA could run the race, exempting the Head of the Charles committee from responsibilities. They called upon their many contacts in Philadelphia's rowing community to make phone calls on their behalf. Eventually, the Head of the Charles board accepted the Aldens, with the proviso that the association would have to allow open rowing shells from other manufacturers to participate in the Alden race, even though they would race in categories separate from the Aldens. Furthermore, the Alden race would have to start at seven in the morning, before the start of the main event.

The Alden race, now known as EBRoC, the acronym for the Ernestine Bayer Race on the Charles, has been held each year since 1972. No one has complained; however, a few years ago the Head of the Charles committee had to limit the numbers of competitors to sixty so that the other races could run on time.

Recalling her triumphant effort for admission to the Head of the Charles during an interview in 2000, Ernie said, "It was really an accomplishment to be admitted. They were great people, but they didn't know much about the Aldens. But they pulled it off for me."

Abby Peck, the Wellesley College women's coach, said she was not at all surprised that Ernie embraced the Alden opportunity after years of exposure to the boathouse racing shell culture. "It didn't matter," she said, referring to the stubby little Alden single. "Ernie really embraced the essence of rowing, and part of that essence is the rhythm of the rower's body in the water, sharing the motion and the magic of what is happening. The people who row Aldens are just as much in touch with that magic as anyone else. Rowing touches something that is essential in each of us and you can plug into it whether you are in a high-end racing shell or an Alden.

"Because the magic of rowing could happen, no matter what the shell, Ernie was following a natural flow from starting a competitive rowing club in Philadelphia to starting the AOSA. I have known a lot of rowers who think rowing is all about high-speed competition but they miss the essence of the sport. To exclude a whole realm of people who participate in this sport because they row Aldens is both shortsighted and limiting. Ernie knew this."

Once Ernie took hold, the AOSA "grew like topsy," said Marjorie Burgard. "Ernie had connections. She grabbed the ball and ran with it. Without her we would not have gotten into the Head of the Charles. She was tireless. I don't think anyone but Ernie could have developed the AOSA the way she did. She was a terrific saleswoman. She could sell ice to Eskimos," she said.

"Because of Harry Parker, the Harvard coach who had helped us, and Ernie, we began to pick up customers from the other rowing world," said Burgard. "Many of them were former college or club rowers who had summer places in New England and wanted a no-care shell so they could continue to row. The AOSA became a cheering section for the Alden shells and Ernie was the biggest cheerleader."

"She was also one of the prettiest scullers I had ever seen. She had a beautiful, smooth stroke, whether she was in a scull or a sweep shell. She became my mentor, teaching me how to use a racing shell. There may be many women who can row as well as Ernie but I don't think any of them can row any better than she can."

"We gave her an experience in ocean rowing," she continued, "and she found that the skills needed to row in the ocean were a surprise to her. She came to respect the ocean rowers just as she respected the premier rowers in Philadelphia."

Single scullers line up for start at Carnegie Lake Regatta, 2005.   Jack Lowe

CHAPTER 16:

__TITLE IX__

Ernie and Title IX made it possible for these girls to compete in rowing. Lew Cuyler

I N SOME RESPECTS ERNESTINE BAYER IS LIKE JOHN THE BAPTIST. From 1938 to 1972 she was the voice crying in the wilderness about the possibilities of women's rowing. She fought against tremendous cultural odds to attract women to the sport, and to show them how to row and how to compete.

However, in spite of her efforts, women's rowing would never be where it is today without the passage of Title IX of the Education Amendments of 1972, the primary law barring sex discrimination in all facets of education, including sports programs.

The law was clear. To be eligible for federal grants and other financial support, schools and colleges had to offer sports programs for women that would equal those for men in opportunities for participation and in the facilities offered.

The legislation had a particular impact on the larger colleges and universities in the US, particularly those supported by

public money. For the most part their big athletic programs were football, basketball, and baseball—for men. These all required supporting facilities. And they all had paybacks through the sales of tickets for major games and for the opportunity they offered for alumni support.

Now they had to create the same opportunities for women. Crew was a natural because it would absorb so many women and because the facilities—boathouses, shells, training equipment and other infrastructure—were already in place for the men's programs and could be used equally by women.

The result was that women were encouraged to participate in rowing and, in fact, offered scholarships to do so, because attracting them to crew was the easiest way to satisfy the Title IX requirements. Crew turned out to be a wonderful fit for women. Perhaps even more than men, they took to the bonding that is part of the sport. They liked teamwork. The sport also gave taller girls pride as they found that height and long limbs were a particular asset.

In August 2002, the National Women's Law Center issued a summary report on the law spelling out what had been done, and what needed to be done.

In a summary paragraph, it reported, "Since its passage 30 years ago, Title IX has led to greater opportunities for girls and women to play sports, receive scholarships, and obtain other important benefits that flow from sports participation. In 1972, fewer than 32,000 women competed in intercollegiate athletics. Women received only 2% of schools' athletic budgets, and athletic scholarships for women were nonexistent. Today, the number of college women participating in competitive athletics is nearly five times the pre-Title IX rate. Title IX has had tremendous impact on female athletic opportunities at the high school level as well. Before Title IX, fewer than 300,000 high school girls played competitive sports. By 2001, the number had climbed to 2.78 million."

Put another way, Title IX validated Ernestine Bayer. She was the forerunner.

In recent years, Title IX has been under siege. Some schools have dropped longstanding programs for males in order to meet Title IX requirements, prompting controversy from alumni and former athletes. It led *US News and World Report* to report in a cover story in 2002 that "the notion that gender equity can mean adding women's opportunities at the expense of those for men has now embroiled conservatives, women's rights advocates, coaches, administrators, and the athletes themselves in a bare-knuckle brawl. Some call this a new 'quota system.'..."

Whatever happens to Title IX in the next few years, it will not take away what has already been accomplished: producing thousands of women rowers and making their participation in the sport totally legitimate.

Ernestine Bayer did not create Title IX. However, she laid the groundwork, and when Title IX was passed, there was already a foundation in place for women rowers. Ernestine had built that foundation. Title IX made the rest happen.

CHAPTER 17:
THE UNIVERSITY
OF NEW HAMPSHIRE

SHORTLY AFTER ERNIE UNDERTOOK THE START-UP OF THE Alden Ocean Shell Association, she became involved with another start-up: women's rowing at the University of New Hampshire in nearby Durham, only a few miles away from her home in Kittery Point.

The Alden Ocean Shell Association was a piece of cake compared to the women's rowing start-up at the University of New Hampshire. There were far more people involved at UNH, there was no equipment, no administrative office facility, and no funding, but there were women who wanted to row.

It all started with Jim Dreher, a nationally-ranked rower. Today he is president and founder of the Durham Boat Co. in Durham, NH, the hometown for the university, Jim had owned a small auto parts company in Detroit. He was a member of the Detroit Boat Club, and had successfully coached crews in his spare time, oarsmen whose boats won US and Canadian championships.

He moved to New Hampshire in the late 1960s, having sold his business in Detroit. At that time, there was no rowing in the state, but Jim had brought some shells along with him. During his first winter he explored the possibilities of rowing in coastal waters, investigating ocean inlets on his cross-country skis. He had dreamed of starting a rowing club for the townspeople of Durham, complete with a boathouse.

That dream began to materialize when the University of New Hampshire decided to start a rowing program and called upon

Jim to guide the effort. At the start of the 1973 academic year, the first meeting was held. Sixteen oarsmen showed up—enough for an eight and a four—as well as five women, including Liz Hills, later to be the highly-respected Radcliffe coach.

The turnout was more than Jim had expected. He had the equipment and time for the men's four and a men's eight, but what about the women?

"I had neither the time nor the energy," he said.

He knew Ernest Bayer by reputation. He had also learned that Ernest and his family had just moved to Kittery Point, ME, not far from the UNH. So he called to see whether Ernest might be interested in coaching five girls.

"I am not," Ernest said, "but my girls might be."

They were.

"The next day," Jim said, "the three Bayers and their dog showed up."

The university women, none of whom had ever rowed, were to share the four with the men. The four was a boat that Jim had rescued on its way to a bonfire. He had been on the Boston University campus right after the Head of the Charles race the year before and had spotted a group of students carrying a wooden four somewhere.

He asked them where they were going.

"We plan to use it for a bonfire," they said.

"Oh, no," he said. He persuaded them to load it on his car.

"It was quite a shell," said Tina. "It was so loose it actually shimmied in the water so you never knew how your oar was going to enter the water because its sides flexed so much. But the point was that it floated, and for us, that was all that counted."

First, however, the Bayers had to teach the girls how to row. They knew they could not put four girls who had never rowed into a four-oared shell with the fifth as cox. So the Bayers brought the two Alden Oarmasters from their double for the first formal practice.

"We put a port oar in one; a starboard oar in the other," said Tina. "And that's how we started: rowing the Oarmasters on the grass. We probably taught five women and ten men that first day."

One of the rowers, Liz Hills, showed unusual talent. Both Ernie and Tina were amazed the first time they saw her row on the Oarmaster. Her form was flawless. They could not believe she had not rowed before.

Hills said she was not surprised at all.

"I have always been drawn to water," she said. "I was a sailor and I knew some of the guys on the men's crew and they said I should try rowing. So I went to the Learn to Row session and watched Ernie and Tina demonstrate. They had the Oarmasters on the grass and were demonstrating the feather. I knew how to feather an oar because my Dad had taught me when I was a little girl. I had also rowed dories a lot."

The coaching progressed. Tina and Ernie introduced the women, three at a time, to the four. They had no coach-boat. Sometimes Ernie coxed and Tina was the fourth rower; sometimes Tina coxed and Ernie was the fourth rower. In the meantime, more girls joined the crew until there was almost enough for an eight. Because of Liz's obvious talent, Ernie and Tina decided to make her stroke and, at the same time, decided they would talk to the women about entering an eight in the Head of the Charles later in the fall.

Jim Dreher, they said, was incredulous. So was the captain of the men's team who by virtue of his captaincy was also captain of the women's team. The women would make fools of the university program; they were much too ambitious, the two men contended. But Jim agreed to call a meeting and have the men and women vote on the idea.

"Look," the Bayer women pointed out. "You have to start somewhere. Let's give it a try. We can borrow a coxswain from Philadelphia who knows the course. We have five women. Both of us (Ernie and Tina) can row. That makes seven. All we need is an eighth rower."

To their credit, Jim Dreher and his captain reluctantly approved. Since they would be rowing as a club and not as part of a formal college program, the rules would allow Ernie, Tina, and a borrowed cox to compete. Still, the Bayer-coached crew went through most of the fall with the five student rowers, plus Ernie and Tina. A week before the Charles, they recruited Dizy Burbridge, daughter of Marjorie Martin. She had done some sculling and was doing graduate work at UNH.

"We showed her how to do it with one oar and put her in the six seat," said Tina.

Much to everyone's surprise, the women made a respectable showing in the race, coming in twenty-second out of forty. Tina gave full credit to the coxswain from Philadelphia for their showing. "She knew the course," she said. "She probably cut a half mile off the race for us."

The UNH men were also excited. They also had voted to enter that fall's Head of the Charles. At the time, the two boats the UNH was using, a four and an eight, were being kept on the lawn of one of the UNH professors who lived on the Great Bay where the Atlantic Ocean touches New Hampshire. There was no dock so all crews had to wade into the water to launch the shells. When they returned from practice at high tide one person had to swim the boat closer to the shore so the rest of the crew could get out.

The race also yielded one story that was to be repeated over and over again in the next few years.

Coleen Fuerst, who had rowed in college at Syracuse

and who would subsequently row at the University of New Hampshire—and later marry Jim Dreher—was watching the race with her boyfriend. They were standing on the Eliot Bridge, the last of the seven bridges that shells have to navigate through on the Head of the Charles course.

The UNH women, in a borrowed boat, were wearing navy blue crew-necked sweaters, white turtlenecks, and blue jeans. Except for a bow number, there was no other identification on the boat. Ernie, then sixty-four years old and with flowing white hair, was rowing in the four seat.

"Who are you?" someone yelled down to the University of New Hampshire boat.

"We're UNH," yelled back one of the rowers.

"That's impossible," Coleen yelled back. "Your number four is a little old lady with white hair!"

The story had a happy ending. Coleen's boyfriend, a nationally-ranked rower named Dwayne Hickling, was doing graduate work at the University of New Hampshire. The following Monday he showed up at the women's crew practice. "I want to help coach," he said.

Dwayne's appearance turned out to be a huge asset to such a fledgling program. He had rowed at Syracuse and his connection to the UNH women's crew developed, he became its full-time volunteer coach, providing the leadership needed to make it a competitive team. Along with Jim Dreher and the Bayer women, he was to have a great impact on the early growth of the women's rowing program.

A few days later the women's crew had a second break, the arrival of Gail Ricketson who, with Liz Hills, would go on to row in the 1976 Olympics, part of the US women's eight that won a bronze medal. She arrived at the boathouse on her bicycle a few days after the Charles, as did some other women, just as the fall practice season was ending. "What is this sport? I think I would like to do it. When can I go out?" she asked.

The Bayers invited her to winter practice, which would begin in a few days.

Gail recalled that she had been doing a training ride on her bicycle with several other members of the UNH women's ski team. Tina, she said, was very excited to meet the team members because it gave her the opportunity to recruit athletes from another somewhat related sport. Gail said she was the only one really interested so she returned the next day.

Poppa Bayer, she said, showed her the rudiments of the stroke for about ten minutes on an Alden Oarmaster, and then she was put in the bow of an eight.

"I don't even think it was a full eight," she said. "It was just me, five others, and a coxswain. That was my first true experience in a shell."

The program did not even have a boathouse at the time, Gail said, although one was built by her senior year. As the team wrapped up rowing for the season, the program won permission to store the two shells in one of the buildings on campus, a chicken house. The boats had to be passed up through a second story window. The program did not have a trailer so the crew members walked, carrying the shells the seven miles from Durham Point where they rowed, to the UNH campus and the chicken house.

With the onset of winter, the crew used the University of New Hampshire swimming pool for winter practice. Because of the demands of time on the training facility for the varsity teams, use of the pool had to begin at 4 a.m. and end at 7 a.m. There was some attrition at first because of the early morning schedule, but by this time, word had spread about the sport. Twenty-five women, including Ricketson, showed up for that practice.

The Bayers brought down their Alden double, floated it in the pool, and tied bow and stern to the sides of the pool. Jim Dreher made holes in the oars. Ernie and Tina taught them how to scull. Since there were only had two seats in the double, the girls took turns and then swam laps. Next they went to the weight room and then they went to the indoor track. Men and women practiced together. "It was a total team," Tina said. "It was also nuts."

Gail Ricketson, who had only gone to practices after the Charles, called the swimming pool practices "invaluable."

"Rowing in the pool gave us a sense of power and balance," she said. "We could only make two strokes; then the rope would go taut. At one point Jim Dreher modified an old racing shell and we used that, too. We also learned how to flip the shell and climb back in. That is an important skill which to this day makes me feel safe in a single shell.

"I was athletic and thought I would just love this sport, but even so, going up to the UNH fieldhouse in the dead of winter at four in the morning made me question what I was doing," she said. "I still didn't know what the sport was all about. I did know we had to run stairs, lift weights, then get back on the water. But I didn't know much else."

The winter training in the swimming pool may have been somewhat unorthodox, but bonds grew among the women. The rowing program, such as it was, was a club sport with a budget of only one thousand dollars. By the winter's end everyone, men and women, were treated the same way, and by the spring as boats were put together sometimes men rowed in the women's boats and sometimes women rowed in the men's boats.

Also joining the crew that winter was Coleen Fuerst, who had spotted the lady with white hair rowing for UNH at the Charles regatta.

"Ernie would talk to us about women's rowing and the women who rowed," she said. "At various times we would row in every seat of the boat, bow, stroke, and in between. Ernie would also cox. We were an eclectic group of people…we were pioneers and we came in different sizes. We had to fight for everything we got."

That winter, Jim Dreher approached the town of Durham and asked whether it would donate the use of town-owned waterfront property for the program. He proposed building a boathouse on the land and, in return for the donation, the town would be offered the use of half of the building. The town agreed. Jim then personally arranged for the financing. The resulting building was a Quonset hut with half of its space reserved for the UNH rowing program, and the other half for the town of Durham.

Coleen said the rowing program made them all feel part of the Durham community because of their belonging to a club that was identified with community effort.

"It was a cooperative thing," she said. "We had to build and put in our own docks, for instance. I felt that some of that spirit later was lost as the program became more organized and the University hired coaches who wanted to separate the men's and women's boats."

Despite the efforts during the winter, it did not appear there was enough talent for a women's eight, especially since the fall eight had included a borrowed cox, a borrowed oarswoman, and Tina and Ernie. That meant that any spring eight would have to start from scratch.

Ernie then had another idea.

"Liz Hills and I were just standing there one day late in the winter and Ernie told us we should row a double and go to the Women's Nationals in California to compete," Gail recalled. "We had no idea what a double was. So we said okay…we just did not know what would be involved."

Jim Dreher did know what would be involved and he thought the idea would be impossible. First, Liz and Gail had never rowed a double. Second, they didn't have a boat. Third, they would first have to qualify in the New England regionals in May, and fourth, they could not get on the water until mid-April. Nevertheless, at Ernie's insistence he agreed to coach them, taking turns with Ernest Bayer and Tina Bayer.

There were also two further developments. Liz Hills wanted to continue racing after the Head of the Charles and Tina had begun to think about restarting her rowing career. The two women decided to compete in a double at Philadelphia's Frostbite Regatta, Liz rowing stroke and Tina rowing bow. Liz had no sculling experience so she moved into the Bayer house so she could practice in a single on Chauncey Creek. Ernest Bayer coached them. The first week at the Bayers' Liz rowed Ernie's single with no slide. Ernest stood on the dock and coached her.

When they arrived in Philadelphia they found the only other competition would be Karin Constant and Diane Braceland, both international-level oarswomen who had just returned from both national and international races, including the European championships. "The 1,000 meter race was going to be an absolute travesty," said Tina, "because Karin and Diane had so much more experience, but there we were."

The Constant-Braceland double jumped Liz and Tina by half a length at the start, but then, about thirty strokes into the race, inexplicably stopped.

"UNH, this is your race," said the referee. "Keep rowing."

So Liz and Tina won. After the race, they learned that broken equipment had caused the competing shell's abrupt stop.

Following the race, Tina made a round of visits to every

boathouse on Philadelphia's Boathouse Row, telling whoever would listen about the UNH program and its need for equipment, particularly oars. She asked each boathouse to donate just one oar. She said it didn't matter what kind of oar, or in what condition. The UNH program, she told them, did not have enough oars to put two eights on the water at the same time. Two of the coaches, Ted Nash, now at the University of Pennsylvania, and Bruce LaLonde, at the University Barge Club, were astounded. Sure, Bruce said he could provide oars, but they were broken, antiques, or both.

"We left Philadelphia with sixty-two oars tied to the top of my van," Tina said. Ted Nash donated the prize oar—a lightweight Pocock sweep in pristine condition.

"Jim Dreher almost fainted when he saw the collection," she reported. "I told him that out of sixty-two, there had to be eight sweep oars the he could use."

"What will I do with the rest of them?" Jim asked. He dreaded the repair job. He just did not have the time to fix up old oars.

"Give them to the kids," said Tina. "They can work on them, sand them, shellac them, and then sell them for a fundraiser."

The problem with the Bayers' idea that Liz and Gail should row a double was that the fledgling UNH program did not have one.

Again, Ernie and Tina did not see that as an obstacle.

Ernie called Fred Emerson in Old Lyme, Connecticut. Emerson, a wealthy businessman and avid rowing supporter, had a deep interest in seeing women's rowing develop in the US. He had played an instrumental role in creating the New England Association of Women's Rowing Colleges.

Fred knew Ernie and how persuasive she could be.

He did not owe her any favors. He had already offered to

give the UNH club two eights provided it could raise $1,000 towards the purchase. When the crew raised the money he gave it back and they then used the gift to buy oars.

Now Ernie was on the phone again. This time, she again told him about the fledgling UNH program and about the promise shown by Liz and Gail.

"Fred," she asked, "do you have a double we can borrow?"

"I do," he said. "It's in Middletown, Connecticut. Here's the number of the boathouse. Tell them I said you can have the boat."

So Tina drove down to Middletown and returned with Fred Emerson's double. That spring, as soon as the ice started to break up, Ernie, Tina and Jim started to coach Liz and Gail in the double. But after seeing them row they knew that the girls would not be able to race it in six weeks.

Jim suggested trying them as a pair. Tina pointed out that the program did not have a pair. Once again, Jim rose to the occasion.

"I have a pair of old eight riggers," he said. "I think I can weld them and we can then use them to make the double into a pair." Then, overnight, he adapted the two riggers and made his idea work. Neither Jim nor the Bayers ever told Gail and Liz that they would be rowing a shell that many consider the most difficult of all to row.

Instead, Liz and Gail had six weeks to learn to row the pair for competition.

The New England Regionals race was in Middletown, Connecticut. The two women launched their shell at seven o'clock in the morning to practice racing starts, and one of the makeshift riggers broke. That might have been the end of it, because on an early Sunday morning in an unfamiliar town, it would have been impossible to find the expertise needed to weld the broken rigger.

Tina, who inherited all of her mother's go-for-it characteristics, was not about to give up because the problem appeared overwhelming. Instead, she raised the hood on their vehicle and removed the radiator hose clamps. "Then," she said, "I made a sleeve for the rigger and clamped the hell out of it."

It worked. Liz and Gail won their race, and could then move to a second regatta in Lowell that would determine who would row in the nationals.

CHAPTER 18:
GAIL AND LIZ

FOLLOWING THE MIDDLETOWN RACE IN THAT SPRING OF 1974, Ernie and Tina rode a rollercoaster of events. Their ride included sharp dips of disappointment, unexpected curves, and pinnacles of success as they nursed the UNH program into real life. In the process, they developed two of its oarswomen into contenders in the 1976 Olympic summer games in Montreal, Canada.

The New England regional race at Middletown was the first of two that spring for Gail and Liz. The first race also sparked a relationship between the Boston University and the UNH crews, thanks to what Tina called "horse-trading." The UNH crew wanted to get its shells down to Connecticut a day early so the crew could row the course before the race. Tina wanted the same arrangement for the boat for Gail and Liz who would row the pair. So she arranged an exchange whereby Gail and Liz could travel with the BU crew, if she and a coach from BU, using Tina's truck-van, drove the trailer with the larger shells.

"Packing them up on the trailer Saturday was a huge amount of work," Tina said, "but the BU coaches, along with some helpers, did it. We started the job at noon on Saturday night and arrived in Middletown, Connecticut at three on Sunday morning. It resulted in that extra day of practice for Gail and Liz and for the BU crew. From then on, we started doing things together." For instance, she said, a few months later, when Coleen Fuerst had joined the crew, she rowed in a combo BU-UNH lightweight eight at the nationals even though she was a UNH student.

Liz and Gail raced again a few weeks later in Lowell, Massachusetts, which resulted in their qualification for national women's competition in June in Oakland, CA. Tina, who was now twenty-nine, and Ernie, now sixty-five, engaged in the cooperative relationship on a much grander scale within days after that race when they again pulled a trailer-load of UNH, BU, and Radcliffe shells across the country to the Women's Nationals. Joining them in the van were Glenn Tyne, an assistant BU coach and Annie Robart, manager of the BU crew. To make sure people knew their cause and destination, Tina decorated her bright yellow tow vehicle with slogans of "Oakland or Bust" and listed the names of every member of the BU and UNH crews who were going to compete. Glenn promised the oarswomen that he had already arranged housing at a friend's "mansion" in Oakland.

The UNH trailer shell-haul arrangement was particularly critical for Liz and Gail, who were rowing the double, now rigged as a pair, borrowed from Fred Emerson. If that shell were not available to them in California, they would have to use a standard pair-oar shell which is equipped with a rudder. This would have confronted them with an entirely new technique— the bow rower using one foot to operate the rudder cables—in a borrowed boat, with no time for practice. They had learned to steer the Emerson shell with their oars and had already successfully raced it twice. Getting that shell to Oakland was key to their being competitive. Gail and Liz were only on the water in the pair for two months prior to the women's nationals. And before the spring, Gail had only rowed in a swimming pool. They had only raced the pair twice, winning both of their events. With that experience behind them, they did not intend to enter national competition in an unfamiliar shell.

Again, timing was important. The original cross-country schedule would have the boats arrive on Friday morning. Tina realized that each day's practice held the key to success. The girls' flight was due to arrive early on Thursday. If the shells could be ready to row on Thursday, all the crews would have an extra day of practice before racing began. Her plan for arrival a day earlier than envisioned meant speeding up the trip.

She presented her idea to the driving crew. Glenn and Annie were supportive but her mother was hesitant. Tina had originally promised Ernie a lovely cross-country trip, dining in good restaurants and staying at nice motels. Making the aggressive timetable work would mean dining in fast food places and sleeping in rest areas or campgrounds.

Tina presented her plan to her mother.

"Well," said Ernie, "Aside from driving and working, what do I get out of this?"

Tina thought about the question for a moment. In a flash, an idea came to her.

"How about an afternoon in Reno, Nevada, playing slot machines?" she replied.

"Okay, I'd like that," said Ernie.

The trip started on a bad note.

The first leg destination was Syracuse, New York, where Ernest Bayer was to be a referee for a major regatta. Bear, the Bayer family dog, joined the four adults in the truck. Before the trip even started, Bear and Annie had taken a dislike for each other, and the truck's close quarters aggravated their respective attitudes. They then all expected to spend the night in a boathouse at Syracuse, but Bear was banned because there was a dog in heat occupying the quarters along with the shells. Instead, the two Bayers and their dog slept in the van, while Annie and Glenn stretched out in the boathouse. Mercifully, the situation did not last. The next day Ernest drove Bear home to Rye.

Nevertheless, the trip still turned out to be the journey from hell.

"Each of the four drivers traded off so we could drive sixteen hours a day," said Tina. "No motels; no fine restaurants. We would pull into a gas station. Then one of us who didn't have to go to the bathroom would gas up, one of us would check the rig, one would go to the bathroom, and the other would get food. Ten minutes, that was it. We spent no more than an hour for dinner at whatever roadhouse we could find that looked cheap and quick. We would pull off at a campground or rest area for a few hours of sleep in the van part of the truck."

They drove through a driving rainstorm on their last night on the road. Visibility was practically nonexistent. Their destination was a campground a mile off the highway. Staying in a highway rest area was out of the question because overnight parking was not permitted.

Around midnight they pulled into the campground with Tina at the wheel. There was no one at the entrance; and virtually no visibility. They saw no other vehicles, not even their lights. Thunder and lightning crashed and flashed around them. Abruptly Tina said, "I can't see a thing in front of me; I am stopping right here."

Despite the storm, Annie and Glenn decided to pitch a tent. Ernie and Tina slept in the truck.

By dawn, the storm had passed, and the sun rose, bright and cheery.

Upon awakening, Ernie and Tina looked out through the windshield. To their amazement, they discovered they had stopped two feet from the lake. If Tina had kept going in the driving rain the night before they would have landed in the lake.

Later that day, only two days after leaving Syracuse, they pulled into a parking lot at a Reno casino. Their sixty-five foot long trailer full of shells took up four parking spaces. The attendant stopped them and said they could not park there.

Tina said, "Then, we will pay for four parking spaces. She explained they planned to play the slot machines for three hours and then leave. The attendant relented and they parked.

The visit was welcome even though they did not win anything. Just playing the slots was fun, and Ernie several times revealed her thrill at the prospect of winning a jackpot.

When they returned to the trailer they found a card under the windshield wiper from a reporter for the "Reno News." The newspaper office was next to the parking lot and the reporter had spotted the rig and immediately sensed the potential for a story. "What are you doing here? Call me," he had written.

Tina and Ernie trooped up to the newspaper office and met the reporter. His story, along with a photo, appeared in the next day's newspaper.

"It was the best write-up about women's crews competing in the nationals that we had ever seen," said Tina.

The next day, they arrived in Oakland only to discover that Snake Drive, the address of Glenn's friend, was on a top of a hill, accessible only by a winding road with cars parked on both sides. Much to their dismay, Ernie and Tina found that the name "Snake Drive" was bulls-eye accurate as they undertook the tricky job of driving the long trailer up the hill and navigating its sharp curves.

It turned out that the "mansion" Glenn had described was really a house with three bedrooms and two bathrooms, quite attractive, but not a mansion. The owners, parents of an infant, had no idea that their conversation with Glenn would result in their housing twenty-two people, plus a van and a 65-foot trailer in their driveway. In fact, they were astounded that the truck-van and trailer had even made it up the hill. Their neighbors came out to gape at the unusual sight. And Tina discovered that the only way to get back to the highway was to back the rig down the mile-long hill. There was no turn-around.

Despite the arrival of their surprise guests with more to come, Glenn's friends were very welcoming. They explained that they only had one bedroom to spare, but the rowers could also sleep on the floor of the family room and on their outdoor screened porch. They said they were leaving the next day for a vacation in Hawaii and gave Tina the keys to their house. After they left and he had seen the situation, Dan Backinowski, the BU coach, found a local rental establishment where he rented cots for everyone.

The hosts imposed one condition: their dog could not leave the fenced-in yard, because he always ran away. "The gate must always be closed," they said. Then they left.

Almost immediately there was a crisis. The dog escaped. Annie had inadvertently left the gate open as she and Tina were unloading the van. Tina took off running after the dog, knowing she did not have a name, address, or phone number to call to see whether anyone had spotted the escapee. She searched the unfamiliar neighborhoods, asked questions, became lost. Then someone recognized the dog and gave her and dog a ride back. By the time she had returned, everyone had gone to bed.

"Mom was furious and frightened," she said. "No one knew where I was."

The next day, Tina and Ernie drove the trailer to the venue and unloaded the shells. They met the BU/UNH crews at the airport, triumphantly telling them that the shells awaited them, the lodging was arranged, and the crew could practice that afternoon. It was mission accomplished for the cross-country trip.

Gail and Liz both rowed in the finals for the Novice Wherry classification. At the start, Gail caught a crab on one stroke, trapping her oar under water, and the resulting leverage from the oar handle almost threw her out of the boat. Liz saw the mishap and told herself, "Dammit, I have to win this race because Ernie told me one of us had to." She did.

After the race, Tom McKibbon, who coached scullers at Long Beach, asked Tina where Liz had come from and how long had she rowed. She was a great sculler, he acknowledged, but he would probably have to lodge a protest because she had been rowing for more than a year and the wherry race was for novices.

"No, she never rowed before last fall," Tina assured him. "Before this spring, when she rowed a pair, she rowed an Alden Ocean Shell in a swimming pool. She rowed all winter that way."

"That's hard to believe," the official said. "She just beat the top novice sculler on the west coast."

The two BU boats, both of them fours, also triumphed, winning both the lightweight and the heavyweight finals. *The Oarsman* reported that the two boats coached by Dan Bakinowski and Andy Bowers "accomplished this feat despite a strong four-oared field, perhaps the most evenly balanced group in the regatta."

Liz and Gail teamed up for the pair. They were to row against Ann and Marie Jonik from Vesper in Philadelphia, identical twins who were beautiful rowers, both physically and in their technique, which was so matched that they could row their pair as if they were a single person. The Joniks won, but were disqualified because they rowed out of their lane and then collided with Princeton. The regatta officials met immediately to discuss the situation and ordered a re-row, but refused to allow the Joniks to compete. Princeton won the five-shell event, earning the right to compete in the FISA world championships in Lucerne, Switzerland, in the early fall. Liz and Gail were second.

Liz Hills O'Leary, now the Radcliffe coach and regarded as among the top coaches in the US, recalled that Ernie rushed up to her right after the race.

"Great row," she said with obvious excitement. "You came in second. That means you made the national team as spares. This will be your big chance, your big opportunity."

"Gail and I just looked at her in amazement," Liz said. "We didn't know what she was talking about. National team? Spares? Going to Lucerne, Switzerland for the world championships? We had no idea national team selections were going on. We didn't have a clue."

Ernie said they would have to spend the summer in Boston training for Lucerne.

But Liz already had a summer job, teaching sailing on Cape Cod. Everything was all set. No, she did not want to spend the summer in Boston.

Ernie was upset and disappointed. "You are ruining your career," she declared. "You'll have the chance to be on the 1976 national team for the first Olympics for women rowers. You can't pass this up."

"I'm a Taurus, I'm a sailor, and I'm stubborn. I stuck to my guns and told her I wasn't going to spend the summer in Boston," Liz concluded. "She was not at all happy about that."

Gail, however, jumped at the chance. She accepted the Bayers' invitation to stay at their house in Rye and spent about ten days with them, primarily doing dry land training and seeking financial assistance from the UNH. She then moved to Boston to train with the BU women and to work at a printing business between practices. Before leaving for Lucerne later in the summer, the BU four, Gail, and another spare revisited the Bayers for a change of scenery. They brought shells. Training with them from a second four during that stay were Tina, their coaches, and Gail.

"It was an amazing summer," Gail said. "The Bayers were incredibly nurturing, giving me unconditional support for my rowing. While my interactions with Ernest Bayer were never as many as with Ernie and Tina, he, too, was warm and welcoming.

I will remember him most for his gentle ways, our conversations, and his stories about the 1928 Olympics."

Gail did go to Lucerne as a spare for the BU shell. And although she did not have the opportunity to row, "for me it was a real eye-opener and probably the turning point in my rowing career. I came back and said I really want to do this sport."

In the meantime, Liz followed through on her sailing job, then returned to UNH for her senior year and the fall rowing season. But then, she said, she withdrew from school for the spring semester and moved out to Long Beach, California to join the scullers working with Tom McKibbon to train for the Olympics.

"It was all Ernie's doing," she said. "Ernie got to me in the fall when I returned to school, and it was the best thing that had happened to me at UNH. I loved the Bayers and I had been a successful rower. Ernie may have scolded me and she may have been disappointed in my decision to be a sailing instructor, but she did not give up on me."

CHAPTER 19:
NOTTINGHAM AND
THE RED ROSE CREW

MANY PEOPLE IN THE ROWING WORLD ARE FAMILIAR with the story of the Red Rose Crew, an unlikely women's eight that came within a hairbreadth of beating the mighty East Germans, losing by a scant 1.6 seconds in a six-boat 1000-meter FISA world championship race held in Nottingham, England. The performance was totally unexpected because it was so unlikely. In fact, however, it demonstrated in dramatic fashion that the underrated US women were going to be serious challengers in the 1976 Olympics.

Daniel J. Boyne, director of recreational rowing at Harvard, tells the story in gripping detail in his classic work "The Red Rose Crew," published in 2000. The account was about eight women rowers and their coxswain, each a bit of a rebel and each with an edge. Under Harvard coach Harry Parker's guidance, they managed to perform an alchemy on their individual gritty personas and became a boat that surprised the world.

The performance of the Red Rose Crew—named because one of the managers had laced a red rose into each of their shoes for good luck in the final—contained the stuff of athletic lore for the ages, and, in its way, is comparable to the US beating the Russians in hockey in the 1980 winter games.

Earlier in 1975, Tina had accepted the job as manager for the team, and she and Ernie had gone to Nottingham to prepare for its arrival and to take care of the team's arrangements during the regatta. It should have been a dream job, but in fact it turned out to be a nightmare of poor organization salted with what the Bayers perceived as the misbehavior of some of the oarswomen. Tina described the Nottingham experience as "just awful... everyone was quick to blame, quick to criticize, and nobody wanted to do the work."

The Nottingham organizing committee did not have the logistics in place for the crew's arrival—there were no beds, no transportation, and no meals. That, combined with what the Bayers perceived as inappropriate behavior on the part of oarswomen representing the United States, soured the experience.

The gaps in the planning process, Tina said, meant that "Mom and I cooked and made beds for a crew of thirty-five people. We found vans for both the women's and lightweight men's teams, and we arranged all transportation because the promised bus transports were not available."

She said she was not able to do her job as manager "because I was doing all the stuff that should have been done by the organizing committee." For instance, equipment didn't arrive on time, and her mother had to make a special all-day trip to Heathrow Airport in London to pick up slides that should have arrived with the shells.

In addition, she said, the sculling team, which had toured Europe with its own manager racing several regattas prior to the European Championships, was supposed to cable its arrival date and time. Instead, the scullers arrived unexpectedly two days prior to their earliest arrival date at the regatta site. That meant that she immediately had to make arrangements for two more vans, as well as procure and make up beds for the entire sculling contingency.

At the end of the competition, Tina encountered another surprise: she was to prepare the shells for shipment back to the

United States. Since they were fragile cargo, she had to obtain bubble plastic wrapping, and then she, her mother, and Evelyn Bergman, a rower friend, carefully wrapped each shell. She then had to meet the shipment in the US, pay people to unload the shells, and then transport them to Radcliffe. Every boat arrived safely with no damage.

In contrast, professionals handled all of the transportation for the men's team. Even so, she said, two of the men's shells were badly damaged and had to be replaced. The final straw, she said, was that the rowing authorities in charge of the US team criticized her for the way she had packed the boats.

Boyne wrote that discipline regarding training became an uncomfortable issue for the Bayers. He reported that Ernestine "did not like some of the things she saw happening with Parker's crew, like the evening revelry of certain rowers. ... In an effort to put a halt to this, she tried to institute certain 'training rules' among them, and even set up her room nearby and left her door open to ensure these were followed. Rowers were required to sign out of their dorms and report exactly where they were going."

Tina said that the girls grumbled and acted as if they were following the rules, but then some of them climbed out of a window to enjoy their free evening time. She and her mother had strong feelings about what they perceived to be unacceptable behavior between some crew members and their boyfriends. "These women represented the United States," Tina declared, "and both of us believed that they should have put their personal lives aside while they were in uniform."

The tension betrayed the classic conflict between generations. Attitudes toward sex and other types of behavior had undergone profound changes since Ernie was a young woman. At Nottingham, Ernie's age was sixty-six, and her values were traditional, even though she and Ernest, in their ways and at an age similar to the Red Rose Crew members, challenged authority in 1928, when they secretly married before the Olympics. The Red Rose Crew oarswomen were in their twenties, and belonged to a generation used to pushing the envelopes of authority. And authority, for them, included Ernie and her rules. So they butted heads. Ernie was strong-willed and older. Members of the Red Rose crew were equally strong-willed but younger. They perceived Ernie as being a bit old-fashioned.

The upshot was that Harry Parker told her to ease up.

Commenting on the situation from the perspective of 2006, Dan Boyne said that the feisty women of the Red Rose Crew were too young to have shared in the traditions of rowing that included training rules because they weren't part of the sport until Ernie came along. "Instead," he said, "they had scratched their way up into the sport and as a result they believed their behavior was not subject to the old rules."

In its way, the episode at Nottingham was similar to what had happened to Ernestine at the PGRC at the end of the 1960s, when discontent surfaced among the younger rowers who were upset over the rules that Ernie had decreed. In both cases, the Bayer women had grown accustomed to their activist roles in campaigning for the acceptance of women's rowing. They had started a revolution in rowing, but by the end of the 1960s, the times were such that the representatives of the culture they had started—the young women—were now rejecting the "old school" discipline that the Bayers still tried to impose.

CHAPTER 20:
THE 1976 OLYMPICS

TINA WAS NO LONGER CONTENT TO BE ON THE SIDELINES. She decided to try out for the 1976 Olympics in singles. She trained that fall in New Hampshire, and then in the spring of 1976, quit her job and moved to Philadelphia to train with Gail Ricketson. In June, she went out to California to prep for the sculling trials and try-outs for the Olympic training camp.

But it was not to be. She and Karin Constant, her rower friend from Philadelphia, were bypassed for the Olympic training camp. Neither made the initial cut of the top fourteen, yet both finished ahead of two others selected. Karin and Tina approached the US Team sculling coach and asked permission to stay on in Long Beach and train in a double, with the idea of challenging the eventual camp boat in the trial to be held later that summer. For various reasons, some of them murky, that effort was frustrated.

Karin and Tina were in an awkward position. Karin's husband, Gus Constant, and Tina's mother, Ernestine, were both members of that first women's Olympic Committee. Karin and Tina decided they should head home, present their case to the Olympic Committee and see whether it would support their challenge of the eventual camp double. The US Women's Olympic Rowing Committee agreed, but the Committee's chairman dissented. Then the US Olympic Committee, which had final authority on the issue, upheld the recommendation of the dissenting chairman and overruled the earlier approval of the US Women's Olympic Rowing Committee.

"For whatever reason, politics was at work," Tina said, expressing her bitter disappointment. "We could have gone to court, but decided against it. Karin and I then raced in a double on the Fourth of July in Philadelphia and won by four lengths. And that was the end of my rowing career."

Sadly, the end for Tina coincided with the ascendancy of US women Olympic rowers, which started in 1976 with two medals, continued in 1984, when the women's eight won a gold, and in 2004, when it took a silver. American women also medaled in singles, double sculls, and pairs in 1988, 1992, 1996, and 2000.

In 1976, the debut for women's Olympic rowing competition, the US eight celebrated with its win of a bronze medal. Joan Lind, a sculler from Long Beach, California, then added to the luster by winning a silver medal in the singles event.

Collectively, those medals added up to a huge gold medal for Ernestine Bayer. Only nine years before, she had struggled against huge obstacles to take American women to Vichy, France for their first international competition. It was a time when women rowers were not yet admitted to the Olympics. Now, at sixty-seven years old, she could rejoice—the women's performances had validated her deep convictions about women's rowing in the United States.

She was also personally invested in the games, first because in 1975 she had accepted an appointment as a member of the first United States Women's Olympic Rowing Committee, and second, because she was responsible for the rowing careers of both Gail Ricketson and Liz Hills. Gail rowed bow in the bronze medal-winning women's eight, and Liz held down the quad's two seat. And although she had not been involved in the career of Joan Lind, she could take pride in the fact that her own pioneering role in the development of women's rowing was a factor in Lind's triumph.

Yet the Olympic experience was bittersweet. She had hoped Tina could compete but she was not in a position to reverse the vote that denied her the opportunity, no matter how much she wished the decision could have been otherwise. She could only join in the praise for the performances of the other US women.

Leading that praise was The *Oarsman*, the official publication of the National Association of Amateur Oarsmen, sponsors for the US Olympic rowers. In a glowing account, it reported that Joan Lind's "superb Silver Medal performance and an extremely strong Bronze Medal row by the eight fulfilled the expectations of many that the women were the United States' best hopes in the 1976 Olympic Games."

The article pointed out that the team demonstrated "the overall strength of US women's rowing," noting that the women's rowing "came from a country that did virtually nothing internationally until 1973." The results represented "an incredible achievement which the entire rowing world has noted and applauded," it concluded.

In the bow seat of the bronze medal eight, Gail rowed with four members of the Red Rose crew, the cox and three oarswomen. They were Wisconsin's Carie Graves, Yale's Anne Warner, Princeton grad Carol Brown and Lynn Silliman, the seventeen-year-old coxswain. The other four rowers were Peggy McCarthy, Marion Greig, Anita DeFrantz and Jackie Zoch. Under windy rowing conditions the US and East Germany took an early lead, followed very closely by Canada and Russia. Russia made its move in the second half but could not catch the East Germans. The US finished third, a little less than a second ahead of Canada.

"It was clear from the beginning of the regatta that both the East German and Russian eights were superb," The Oarsman reported, "and although we were right in the thick of it, it would take a superlative effort to defeat either of them. ... The oarswomen appeared delighted with the Olympic medal, and after the race Harry Parker (their coach) expressed himself completely satisfied. ... To win an Olympic medal at this level of competition is a superlative achievement, and one certainly undreamed of in the US only a couple of years ago."

Gail recalls the crew as being "extremely strong" but needing more long distance training. "If the course had been 500 to 700 meters we might have won the gold," she said, "but we began to die during the final strokes. We just barely squeaked out a victory over the Canadian boat, which really revved it up at the finish. It was a good race overall. When the cox yelled we were ahead I just focused on the back in front of me and making strong, perfect strokes."

Joan Lind was already well-known in the rowing community, having been the first woman ever to grace the cover of *The Oarsman*, in 1973 after she won the US single sculling championship at the age of twenty.

The Oarsman reported that Lind's race was particularly dramatic. She "blasted right out, and appeared on TV to be second, just a bit behind Scheiblich (the East German) after the first five strokes. But in the next few strokes, she fell to fourth, although everything was still very tightly bunched. And then came one of the most beautiful sights of the regatta as Joan began to move back through. The Dutch sculler, Munneke, had blasted out to an early lead, hoping to perhaps steal the race. At 250 meters, Scheiblich was second, Antonova third, and Joan fourth, .42 seconds behind the Russian.

"But then, the speed and the power and the form that Joan had worked so long to attain began to tell, as first she caught Antonova and then the already fading Munneke. At 500 meters Joan was second, only .47 seconds behind Scheiblich.

In her third 250, Joan was .92 seconds faster than the Russian, and in the final 250 put even more distance between them by going 1.74 seconds faster; in fact, Joan was .77 seconds faster than Scheiblich over the final 250, and not only had earned herself a silver medal but was actually challenging for the gold. At the finish, Scheiblich had .65 seconds on Joan, which the TV showed to be about two-thirds of a length. Several competitors mentioned that no one had ever made Scheiblich work so hard to win.

"Grinning from ear to ear, a justifiably proud Joan Lind received the first Olympic medal ever won by an American rower. Afterwards, mobbed by well-wishers and a goodly number of the press, she said she had no race plan other than to go out and row as fast as she could."

Liz Hills did not share that degree of glory but was part of a winning race when her coxed quad took a first in the Petite Final, beating both Hungary and Canada. In rowing terms the *Petite Final*, also called *repechage*, is a second chance race between the losers in the earlier heats.

In a postscript to the Olympics, Tina changed her focus from rowing to raising and breeding Belgian Sheep Dogs, an activity she continues to invest with all of the zest she had once reserved for her rowing career.

CHAPTER 21:
SQUAMSCOTT
SCULLERS AND
RECOGNITIONS

Ernie and helper carry Alden back to boathouse after row on Squamscott River.

Charles Came

RNIE WAS SIXTY-SEVEN AS THE OLYMPICS ENDED, A TIME of life when she might have slowed down. Slowing down, however, had never been her style. Instead, she kept up a steady pace as she entered what most people consider the "golden years." Her post Olympic achievements included the founding of still another rowing club and the rowing community's formal recognition of her accomplishments.

In 1976 she spotted an advertisement for waterfront property on the Squamscott River in New Hampshire. She organized a meeting of rowers in the New Hampshire Seacoast area; they accepted her proposal to buy the property and then named themselves the Squamscott Scullers. About the same time, the Bayers built a new home in New Hampshire, on the shore of Squamscott River, only about a mile north of the boathouse.

That meant that Ernie could row a four-mile course almost daily, on her own schedule, an activity she continued into her nineties. As rowing clubs go, Squamscott is quite small, with perhaps a dozen rowers who use it regularly. The boathouse is located on a secluded wooded spot about fifty yards from its dock on a quiet stretch of the river. With no particular programs or aspirations except for rowing convenience for its members, the club has functioned very nicely since the late 1970s without benefit of extensive infrastructure or publicity.

The 1976 Olympics gave both status and validation to competitive women's rowing programs. Women rowers had proved conclusively to the male community that they could row fast, they could work hard to achieve their goals, and that they were as good as those from the much more established women's programs in Europe and other parts of the world.

The ascendancy of women in the sport also prompted more thoughtful rowers to reflect on what had happened. First, many were becoming aware that the 1960s had taken a toll on the sport and it was women who had come to the rescue.

They were discovering that the seeds of freedom of expression and behavior had taken root and blossomed as the 1970s began. As a result they were finding that men with potential for rowing excellence, did not choose to undergo the discipline that the sport demanded. Not only was the training time consuming and exhausting, the demands of the sport to subvert personal expression were unsettling, even out of place in the post-1960s culture. They found that there is truth to the saying that "democracy and freedom of expression find no place in a rowing shell" and that was contrary to their other,

The Three Bayers, Ernestine, Ernest and Tina share happy evening when Ernie was inducted into Rowing Hall of Fame in 1984 in Philadelphia.
Bayer family files

developing, values. The result was a tentative conclusion that rowing might have seen its apex and was now diminishing in popularity as a sport or, as David Halberstam put, "an anomaly, an encapsulated nineteenth century world in the hyped-up twentieth century world of commercialized sports."

Finally, they began to realize that the entry of women may have saved the sport and prevented it from becoming a fossil. The women infused new life and new spirit into a hidebound culture. They began to realize that it was Ernie Bayer who had led the charge and that she should be recognized.

Rowing has some major awards for those who have contributed. One is the John Carlin Service Award.

Carlin, who had initially denied Ernie's attempt to enter a women's shell into world competition in 1967, was nevertheless the most esteemed man in the development of US Rowing. For more than twenty-five years he held office, including the presidency of the National Association of Amateur Oarsmen. He was just as involved in the international aspects of the sport and in one decade made nineteen trips to Europe as the North American vice president for FISA, the sport's international governing organization. He was widely credited with "shaking rowing out of its provincial isolationism to an acknowledgement and acceptance of the challenge of the international rowing community."

He died on Nov. 8, 1968 at the age of seventy-two. Subsequently, the rowing establishment created a service award in his honor to be made each year to the rower whose work most exemplified his contributions to the sport.

In 1980, Ernestine Bayer became the first woman to receive the John Carlin award. To date, she is the only woman to have been so honored. John Kiefer, a Philadelphia rower and a friend of Carlin's for many years, said he firmly believed that despite his early opposition to Ernie's aspirations for women's rowing, John would have been very pleased that she had prevailed and had earned the award in his name.

A second important award is induction into the Helms Rowing Hall of Fame. Instituted in 1956, it was the concept of three men: Clifford "Tip" Goes, Paul H. Helms, and W.R. (Bill) Schroeder. Its objective was to honor distinguished American oarsmen, crews, coaches, and noteworthy contributors to rowing. They were to be nominated by a committee following a review of candidates.

In 1984, Ernestine became the first woman to be inducted into the Hall of Fame during ceremonies in Philadelphia. In doing so, she joined her husband, Ernest, a 1974 inductee as a member of the coxless four that had won the silver at the 1928 Olympics.

In 1992, US Rowing nominated Ernestine for the Sullivan Award, the nation's top amateur athlete award. The nomination was a surprise, especially since Ernie, then eighty-three, was still competing, even though she had to race women at least ten years younger.

In making the nomination, US Rowing said that "Mrs. Bayer has achieved the highest form of amateurism in participating in rowing and sharing it with so many others without any thought of personal gain. Her accomplishments in rowing have been the most pure and truly amateur because all that she did was with the knowledge that she would never realize her goal of representing the United States in the Olympic Games or World Championships."

Sullivan awards had been given since 1930 and over the years had gone to several Olympic notables, including Carl Lewis in track, and Mark Spitz in swimming, figure skater Kristi Yamaguchi, and boxer Oscar De La Hoya, all of them Olympic gold medalists, and all of them much younger than Ernie. It had never gone to a rower, despite rowing's reputation of being the first and last amateur sport.

Against such competition, she wasn't selected. The US Rowing nomination was her honor and the fact that she did not receive the ultimate award "just took the pressure off me," she said.

In 1992, she became the first person to receive the prestigious US Rowing Gold Medal for Lifetime Achievement in all venues of rowing, as a competitor, as a coach, as a mentor, and as a leader. In 1993, she was named the Northeastern University "Coach of the Year," and one of the two Olympic eight-oared shells was named in her honor.

In 1994, the Head of the Charles regatta named her Honorary Chairman, in 1998, she was inducted into the New Fund Hall of Fame, and in 2000, she was named one of the top ten people of the century in American rowing. Later that year, at the 2000 Olympics in Sydney, Australia, the US Olympic Women's single was christened "Ernestine Bayer."

She also came to be popularly known as the "Mother of Women's Rowing in the United States" and then later, the "Mother of Recreational Rowing in the United States." By the end of the 1990s she had received many awards, but each time she expressed surprise at the accolades.

"I never set out to make history," she said. "One thing followed naturally on another, and everything I did, I did simply because I love rowing. I just want others to enjoy what I've enjoyed and get the benefits from rowing that I have. I know I wouldn't be in the shape I'm in today if it weren't for rowing."

At one point she was asked to express in writing her reflections on her own success.

"My dream of women's rowing became an actuality because I'm a 'doer'," she wrote. "I never take NO for an answer when others think it is impossible to attain a goal. It just means that the goal becomes more difficult to attain. My goal for women's rowing at a competitive level was realized without my ever expecting recognition for my individual efforts. 'Success' in the world of rowing came to me, I believe, because my own personal goal was achieved.

"I live my life one day at a time, approaching each one with the burning desire to always do my best. (Sometimes I fall flat on my face!) I'm very competitive but my strongest opponent is myself.

"Success? Achieving whatever is one's goal in life."

Ernest and Ernestine, 1980.   National Rowing Foundation

CHAPTER 22:
STILL COMPETING...
STILL WINNING

By the late 1980s, Ernie had become a legend. Her so-called golden years also provided plenty of opportunities for competition. Ernie continued to build the Alden Ocean Shell Association which meant that at first, anyway, she helped organize most of its regattas. And then, of course, she competed in them. Most of the time, she won medals. In 1988, she resigned from her job as secretary of the AOSA, deciding that it took too much time away from what she really wanted to do: row competitively in the years she had left. She was about to turn eighty years old.

The Alden competitions differ markedly from the rarified, high-pressure Olympic, national, and world events.

Ernie sets world record for her age group at Concept 2's CRASH B indoor rowing competition in Boston in 2000.   Bayer Family files

Alden rowers, for the most part, are those who regard themselves as people first, and rowers second, rather than the other way around. They have lots of races, but the atmosphere is much more informal, and fellowship is just as important as racing. With their vast collective experience, Ernie, Tina, and occasionally Ernest could coach, race, and hold clinics for an appreciative group.

Racing for older people, including the Alden rowers, also has advantages in time allowances. The older rowers are awarded an age adjustment, sometimes called a handicap. Essentially, it means that past a certain age, fifty or sixty for most races, for every year that you advance, you receive a head start, in rising increments. For instance, some races give you two seconds per year, others, four seconds. In other words if you are seventy years of age, you might start a race with a thirty-six second advantage.

185

Ernie in bow and Karin Constant stroke to first place in 2002 FISA world competition in Montreal, Canada. Ernie was 92.   Bayer Family photo.

That means that the younger competitors must overcome that thirty-six second lead before they are tied with you, and to beat you, they must win by more than that.

Put another way, the oldest folk may have more than a minute just by rowing to the starting line. Once Ernie was in her seventies and eighties, she had a very distinct time advantage. Ernie also found herself enjoying the Alden double, in which she could stroke but didn't have to navigate. She could pair up with a much younger rower who could keep the shell on course while Ernie did what she always did best: row a smooth stroke for the bow rower to follow.

The upshot was that the older she became the better Ernie was apt to do in races, particularly those of the Alden variety. However, she also occasionally returned to racing shell competition. In 1989, she rowed in the FISA world masters regatta. In 1991, at the age of eighty-two, she and her partner,

Harold Finnegan, won a mixed doubles race at a masters regatta in Florida where she also rowed a single. In 1992, at eighty-three, she rowed to a first at the Head of the Charles in the singles category for women sixty and over. Through 1996, she continued to race at the Head of the Charles and then in the annual US Rowing national regatta.

In 1996, the Head of the Charles Committee denied her the opportunity to race in the singles event because her time the previous year was not fast enough to qualify for automatic entry. Instead, along with hundreds of others, she had to depend on a lottery system for selection.

"It was very unfortunate, but she wasn't alone," said Fred Schoch, race director. He said almost five hundred crews and 265 individual scullers were turned away that year. "I tip my hat to her. We all do," he continued. "She's really an icon in the sport of rowing."

The denial did not keep Ernie out of the Head of the Charles. In 1997, she raced in a double and came in fifth. She continued to race in the double at the Charles through 2001.

"That was typical Ernie behavior," said Jeanne Friedman, who was her doubles partner in one of those races. "She wanted to row in the Head of the Charles, but they wouldn't let her. So she found a way to row at the Charles in a double."

During the 1990s Ernie also rowed in the winter on the Concept 2 Ergometer, a rowing machine. In the year 2000, at the age of ninety-one, she surprised everyone by rowing a measured 2000 meters at the Concept 2 Crash B competition in Boston in twelve minutes and 7.5 seconds. In doing so she set a world record as well as winning the traditional Golden Hammer award for her performance.

She then went on to put on an amazing rowing performance in September 2001 at the FISA World Masters Championships in Montreal, Canada. She was ninety-two years old. She rowed in the Women's Eight, consisting of much younger women, which took a first in its race. The youngest rower, Kate Godwin, was sixty-one. The next oldest to Ernie was Nel Braudsma, was seventy-six.

She and her partner, Karin Constant, also won the women's double. They were the only one in their age group, so the win was automatic. However, they also beat another shell with much younger racers, and without using their handicap.

She also took second in the mixed double category. She and her partner Mike Shields, fifty-three, from the Amoskeag Rowing Club in Manchester, New Hampshire, finished half a length behind Marj and Ralph Burgard. The Burgards had leased a double for the summer and then had gone to a rowing camp for coaching. In contrast, Ernie and Mike just hopped into a borrowed boat at the dock and then rowed to the starting line without benefit of rigging changes, except for a foam pillow that Ernie had decided would be kind to her bottom. They were second out of four shells, even without the age adjustment.

Because of her age, she increasingly attracted press coverage including interviews on CNN and articles in several magazines.

Ernie dismissed the notoriety. "It's simply because I'm old," she said, grinning for emphasis. "Part of the fact that I am able to do these things today is because I've been active all of my life. With the exception of giving birth, I've always rowed."

CHAPTER 23:
CARIE GRAVES
TO THE RESCUE

ERNIE WAS EIGHTY-SEVEN YEARS OLD AND ONE OF the competitors in the 1996 Masters National Championships on Lake Onondaga in Syracuse. Racing conditions were somewhat rough but manageable earlier on Saturday, but had deteriorated by the late afternoon. On Sunday the lake was awash in chop and becoming worse as the wind picked up.

Carie Graves—six seat in the 1976 Olympic bronze medal-winning women's eight, and four seat in the 1984 Olympic gold medal-winning women's eight—teamed up with Landon Carter in Sunday's double sculls event.

Carie was stroke of the Red Rose Crew when she met Ernie in Nottingham in 1975—under somewhat tense circumstances, when Ernie and Tina were acting as shepherdesses for the women at that event. Prior to the Red Rose Crew, Carie had rowed at the University of Wisconsin, so she and the Bayers had not moved in the same circles. "I never really knew her at Nottingham," Carie said. "I did wonder about her at the time. But I had another agenda and she was not part of it. I knew she had been very involved with rowing, and that was about it."

The shells could not engage in warm-up practice because it was so windy. They were all clustered around the start, fours, doubles and singles, awaiting their respective races.

One of the singles flipped. "I knew immediately it was Ernie Bayer," recalled Carie, "and no one else was doing anything. It was as if they were frozen in time. No matter the situation, I don't freeze, I just go for it, for better or for worse.

"I told Landon, 'That's Ernie, I gotta go.'"

Ernie was going under. In rowing terms the accident was somewhat unusual. Because of their enclosed decks, single rowing shells become flotation devices when they flip, so lifejackets have not been required for rowers. However, when the shell flipped Ernie had become separated from the craft, and because of the choppy conditions she could not regain a handhold.

"The lake closed over her head once, twice. She was fighting back as she had always fought for what she wanted; this time kicking, grappling, desperately trying to get hold of the slippery boat from which she had fallen. But the will of the water, dragging her down, seemed stronger than even her own," reported Barbara Huebner the next day in the *Boston Globe's* account of the accident.

Carie was seventy-five meters away. At six foot one, she was able to stand in the shallow water. "Sometimes I was swimming, sometimes I was trying to run through the water to get to her," reported Carie. "It seemed I would never get there in time ...it seemed like total slow motion but it was happening quickly."

By the time Carie reached her, Ernie had gone down for the third time.

"I reached out for her. I said 'It's okay, Ernie. It's me, Carie.' Because of the depth of the water, I could stand and hold her. I still didn't know her, but I did know she was eighty-seven and still rowing and I had tremendous respect for her.

"I had both my arms around her, and I remember her saying, 'Oh, Carie, thank God you are here.' She later told people she was drowning and I had saved her life."

Minutes after the rescue, "a bunch of launches came and there was screaming and confusion," Carie said. "A four had also flipped. The regatta was being halted. A launch took care of Ernie and then I had to get into another launch. I hoisted myself up over its sides and landed in a heap on the bottom of the boat, and ended up with a lot of bruises. I never could have done that under normal conditions. It was all adrenalin."

CHAPTER 24:
"THE MOST UNFORGETTABLE ROW OF MY LIFE"

1984 Olympic Gold Medal women's eight goes out for early morning row on Schuylkill in Philadelphia, with Ernestine Bayer, 75 years old, second from left, as guest of the crew. She is the only one with white hair.   Bayer Family files

ERNIE ONCE SAID THAT SHE HAD NO REGRETS ABOUT being too old to compete in the 1976 Olympics. "I'll never know whether I would have been good enough to compete," she told the *Portsmouth* (NH) *Press* in a 1993 interview. "Of course, if there had been women's rowing early on, there would have been a lot more competition. There just wasn't much when I was competing."

She had laid the groundwork for competitive women's rowing in the United States, but by the time it was established she was too old to compete in the major national and international races. Her only option was to row in seniors events where competition was very limited. The many awards she won late in her life leave us to wonder: How good was she?

Holly Metcalf, a member of the first US women's eight to win an Olympic Gold, in 1984, has offered at least a partial answer. She first met Ernie in Philadelphia, when the women's eight was inducted into the Rowing Hall of Fame, an honor they and Ernie shared that year.

"At that time, I really did not know much about her," said Metcalf. "We wanted to go out for a celebration row the next day, but we had a vacant seat because Carie Graves could not make the ceremony. We decided to invite Ernie to row with us and it turned out that the experience was quite extraordinary."

Metcalf said that she rowed in the two seat and Carie Graves rowed in four, considered a power seat in the "engine room" of the eight. Ernie, she said, did not want to row in the four seat so Metcalf switched and gave her two seat to Ernie.

"We did not expect much," she said. "Carie is six feet one and Ernie is five feet five, so aside from the age difference there was a huge height difference. We decided it would be a paddle and we were going to be nice. We did not want to hurt her. But as it turned out, we were being patronizing."

"We did a few light pieces, and then took a break," she recalled. "After a couple of seconds, Ernie said, 'Come on girls, stop being easy on me. In the next piece, show me your stuff.'"

The comment surprised the crew.

"So we did a few high intensity pieces and we were amazed at how well we made the shell run," Metcalf continued. .

She and the rest of the crew were even more amazed when Ernie said, "Show me again. Let's take a start and ten," meaning ten power strokes.

The crew hesitated but then without speaking to each other

each began to realize that this white haired oarswoman in the two seat felt that they were still holding back and that she wanted them to show real power for the next sequence.

The coxswain gave the command and the crew exploded, each oarswoman exerting maximum power. The shell literally flew through the water as if it had a rocket at its stern. The piece ended, the oarswomen feathered their oars and collectively rejoiced at the power.

"We really could not tell the difference because she was in the boat," Holly said later. " Her stroke was absolutely smooth and she blended in beautifully."

Ernie said that it had been "the most unforgettable row of my life. I have never had such a smooth, powerful row. I cried after the row and I still cry every time I think of it. I've wondered ever since what it would have been like if they had been at full power for more strokes. I was humbled. I had conned them into doing a few racing starts. We took the stroke up three times during three racing starts plus ten power strokes and I don't think I could have taken an eleventh stroke. We were airborne…"

Metcalf was equally moved. "At the time of the row, none of us in the boat really understood how much personal pain she had gone through with the sport of rowing or how she dealt with elements within the rowing community that had ostracized her. She told us during the row that she was not of our caliber. … But she was seventy-five years old and our generation had a different toehold on the sport of rowing.

"Following that row, we all could imagine her as an Olympic athlete, even when she could not see it for herself."

"As for me," she continued, "I finally understood what she made possible."

In later years, Holly became active in promoting women in rowing with a focus on those who were recovering from breast cancer and from abuse.

"My respect for Ernie just kept growing," she said, "Ernie's a purist, someone who exults in the sheer joy of movement. Growing up, she wanted to excel in running or swimming, but she found rowing.

"She just could not help herself. ... The idea that she should encounter opposition in something so pure and so simple as rowing was unthinkable."

A second testimony to Ernie's rowing ability came from Abby Peck, the Wellesley women's coach, who stroked the women's four in the 1984 Olympics and held down the four seat in the 1988 Olympics. She was Ernie's rowing partner in a double in several races during the 1990s.

"Ernie always wanted to do Power Tens," she said. "She was strong, she was smooth, I could follow her, and even though her stroke was not as long as mine, it was rhythmic and it just clicked into the groove. Her set was perfect. She made rowing easy and fun. It was just amazingly deceptive to see this apparently frail woman step into a boat and be transformed right before your eyes into a fiercely competitive athlete."

When Ernestine Bayer had started rowing, the male community was certain that women could never share the exhilaration that came from the power of sending a shell through the water. In the pre-Ernie era of prim and proper women, men questioned how women could possibly understand what rowing was about.

"In my era," Carie Graves said, "women began to experience making a shell go fast and to discover the pleasure of hurting so much—breathing hard, and sweating, and going over the top. Men began to recognize that we could experience the same kind of pain and commitment that they could and that was what Ernie had started....

"The result of Ernie was that we proved to men and to other women that we can do this, that we are tough, and that we are

195

indeed people who can excel in a demanding sport."

Ernie had known this from the first time she saw her husband row. Her row with the 1984 Olympians was an epiphany. "Despite all of the work I had done, I knew that those women in the Olympic gold medal eight were just the beginning and that women had scarcely begun exploring their power through sports.

"They had asked me to row with them and I was honored," she said. "During that row I felt the power of everything I had ever done. It was a payback."

Ernie rowed in the Olympic eight in 1984 with Holly Metcalf as one of the gold medal oarswomen. Several years later Ernie and Holly row a double during Holly's Row As One camp for women at Mt. Holyoke College, South Hadley, MA   Bayer Family files

ERNIE ANECDOTES

Ernie Standing Tall   Charles Came

INTERVIEWED PERHAPS FIFTY PEOPLE IN ORDER TO WRITE THIS account of her life. Many of their stories did not make it into the narrative of the manuscript. But they still need to be told. Among them:

Debbie Arenberg, Director of Recreational Sales, WinTech Racing said she met Ernie in 1979 at a dinner party at a time "when I didn't know anything about the rowing world. However, within five minutes I knew she was pretty special." Ernie saw Debbie's size—nearly six feet and then weighing nearly 200 pounds—and persuaded her to go to the indoor rowing try-outs at Harvard's Weld Boathouse. "Ernie had never seen me row and I didn't know anything. But I went and when I arrived at the boathouse there were female athletes there like I had never seen in my life. I was blown away."

However, she said, it was her introduction to rowing. From then on Ernie kept urging her to try out for the Olympics. However, her life took a different turn of marriage, children, and a career of in the rowing industry. For many years she was the sales manager for Alden Rowing and in 2005 she accepted her current position at WinTech. She never became an Olympic rower but that dinner party meeting with Ernie shaped the rest of her life. Today, like Ernie, she is a missionary who has urged hundreds of people of people to try the sport and then has coached a goodly number of them..

Richard Kuhn, Durham, N.C. said that in the 1940s, he was on the Penn Charter crew in Philadelphia that was coached by Ernest Bayer. "Ernestine was always somehow there and we had a lot of parties and picnics. She loved us all. I went to college but did not row, then I went into the Navy and then I worked for my father in real estate and never did get back into a rowing shell. In the 1980s, I was living in Florida and she was down there and caught up with me. Hands on her hips, she said, 'What excuse do you have now? You can row twelve months a year in this weather.' So I tried a rec shell, then bought an Alden double. Now I live in Arkansas and row every day that I can. I even taught my wife to row.

"She never quits. From the time I left Penn Charter school, she never quit scolding me for not rowing. When I started again forty-some years later, she was overjoyed. I love it and it has become part of my life, but it took her forty years to get me to do it. She has changed my life around and as a result I am now having a lot of fun.

Abby Peck, the Wellesley rowing coach, who rowed with Ernie at the 2001 Head of the Charles, said that after their shell crossed the finish line, "Ernie turned around to look at me and

she had the most gigantic grin on her face that I had ever seen. She was ninety-two. We rowed to the dock and I took her into the boathouse and when I found that she could not stand up, I realized how fully she had given everything she had to the row and that she was just pleased to her core. She was so satisfied, so elated, I don't think she realized how physically drained she was."

Jack Frailey, who served with Ernest Bayer on the board of the National Association of Amateur Oarsmen, commented, "You just can't turn to anyone else except Ernie to find who was responsible for starting women rowing in the US. She wasn't the best organizer in the world, but she did have a crystal clear view of her personal goals. She could spot opportunity."

Charlie McIntyre of Seattle, formerly a Philadelphia rower who rowed at Penn AC, described Ernie as "a good-looking gal with a tan. ... We all thought she was a 'Boathouse Rat,' and when we saw her coming we'd say, 'She's here again. What's she want now? Last year we gave her a pair of oars.' Young guys like us ... we all liked her. ... She would have made a great politician."

Pat Ferguson, a rowing umpire whose associations with the Philadelphia rowing establishment are extensive, told me, "Nothing Ernie did ever surprised me. That Alden thing in New England, for instance. She was so unique; she knew what she wanted to do and what was important to her and that was she wanted to row. So if it wasn't going to be rowing in Philadelphia, then why not try something new?"

Jim Ramsey, a Dartmouth rower in the early 1960, said he met Ernie at the first National Masters Championships in Boston in September 1981. He had come all the way from Tennessee only to lose in the heats in a chilly day of rain, wind, and minor chop. The loss in the heats meant he was out of the competition and, as a result, he was feeling discouraged.

"Momma Bayer took notice of my misfortune as I was scraping around for anything to row for additional races, and offered herself as a partner for mixed doubles," he said. The mixed doubles were scheduled for Sunday and had attracted a field of top rowing couples. "I'm a known sucker for a dare," he recalled, "But what did we have to lose? It was an awful race. We were one hundred meters behind the pack at the finish. But we finished and I will never forget it.

"At the time I didn't know who Ernestine Bayer was...I didn't even know her name

Somebody remarked that we looked like a 'coxed single' during the race...me a big round 240 pounds rowing like a windmill and her riding it out with blades feathered looking like a little wisp of grey hair. Because she was such a good sport my participation was maximized when otherwise my trip could hardly have been justified.

"Her gumption in just 'going out and doing it' in the face of a void in understanding and appreciation of women who row is a good part of what makes her a special person. Nothing can stop such a person. I am proud to know her."

Ellen Ripper, US Rowing referee and master rower met Ernie in 2001 at the FISA world masters regatta in Montreal, Canada where she had just rowed in two events.

"I watched her being interviewed at the dock after she had just finished a race and I had always wanted to meet her so I knew this was my chance.

"I walked up to her after the interview as she was making her way back and I could only think how tired she must be. But I knew if I did not at least try to meet her, I might never again have the opportunity.

"She was so gracious. I just basically wanted to thank her for what she had done for all female rowers. It meant a lot to me. I know she won't remember the moment. I wouldn't expect her to. But I will."

In 1992 Linda Lewis wrote a book entitled *Water's Edge... Women Who Push the Limits in Rowing, Kayaking & Canoeing.* She selected Ernestine Bayer and three other women to profile, along with the 1984 Olympic Gold Medal women's eight. She reported that Ernie was very disappointed that Tina was nineteen and an athlete, but still had not rowed despite a lifelong exposure to the sport. She knew her daughter was like herself and did not understand the word "No." So she asked Ted Nash, PGRC's new coach to dinner and asked him to remark, somewhat casually, "Now look at your daughter. She's not big enough to be in one of my boats." As I have reported, Tina was very upset about the remark and the next day asked her mother to teach her to row.

When I learned of the Lewis account just before completing the manuscript,

I asked Tina whether she had heard that version the story regarding Ernie's orchestration of Ted Nash's remark.

"No, she never told me," said Tina, "but I wouldn't put it past her."

A month later Ted Nash sold Tina his single.

Tina Bayer was born on Sept. 30, 1945. Ernie created her birth announcement using the metaphor of a rowing regatta in which Ernie had made it to the finish line.

BAYERS' REGATTA

September 30, 1945
Official Program
Under the auspices of
Ernest H. and Ernestine
L. Bayer
Regatta Headquarters
Hahnemann Hospital

Mickey McGrath, who rowed with the PGRC during the 1960s, said "What we were doing was unusual. Women, in those days, for the most part did not do sports. I was different because I played basketball, but really, the opportunities for women in sports were very few. It wasn't just rowing … it was every other sport, too. Women just didn't do sports the way men did."

Ernestine never liked the term "rower" and will roundly criticize me for its overuse in this, her biography. Once, during the Head of the Charles, she was watching the race on a bridge beside two young women. A conversation ensued and they both said they were rowers.

"Rowers," she exclaimed, her voice rising in indignation. "Anybody can row. You are not rowers, you are oarswomen. Don't ever forget that."

They were stunned by the unexpected lecture. But it was not a surprise to anyone who had ever heard her talk about rowing. For her, oarsmen and oarswomen are those who are passionate about the sport. They can row port or starboard, sweep or scull, rough water or smooth. They can repair shells and fix coach-boats, teach, fill in and solve problems. They are very special people and she loves them all.

AFTERWORD

AS THIS BOOK IS BEING WRITTEN, ERNESTINE BAYER, NOW ninety-seven, is experiencing a quiet time in her life. A stroke in March 2003 left her partially paralyzed, and abruptly interrupted the fast-forward pace that she had maintained throughout her life and into the first half of her tenth decade.

Characteristically, she was not to be stopped. She underwent intensive therapy, and six months later was again rowing, but with assistance in getting in and out of the shell. Then, in September 2003, she fractured her pelvis in a fall caused by an automatic door. Again she recovered, this time confining her rowing to her Concept 2 Ergometer. But, in July 2005, a second stroke felled her, robbing her of the ability to swallow, to talk and to walk.

With pragmatism and smoothness honed over decades of teamwork, Tina and Ernie reversed roles. Ernie became Baby Bayer, and Tina became Momma Bayer, taking charge of her mother's recovery.

Tina arranged to do most of her work via computer from home, and then set about re-furnishing their house in Stratham with equipment designed to help invalids and the aged remain mobile and vital. Her acquisitions included a hospital bed, a hoist, and a wheelchair. A small elevator for the wheelchair enables it to descend when leaving the house and then ascend to a specially-equipped van that accommodates both Ernie and the chair, allowing Tina to drive. The arrangement has enabled Ernie to be out and about at least three or four times a week, as she accompanies Tina on errands or goes to medical appointments.

When I arrived for a visit in late March 2006, Ernie's eyes lit up with their old flash, signaling recognition of my presence.

A few hours later, an incident revealed that, while she might be down, she has never lost her fire.

Tina and I had taken her to a restaurant. The three of us were seated, Tina and I in a booth, Ernie at the end of the table in her wheelchair, next to her daughter. Tina and I each ordered a glass of wine, and then we engaged in conversation. Ernie appeared to be taking it all in. Tina and I finished our wine and continued talking while awaiting dinner.

"Did you see that?" said Tina, abruptly interrupting our conversation.

"I did," I said.

"It's amazing," she pronounced.

I had to agree. While we were talking, Ernie had reached for Tina's just-emptied wineglass and gripped it by the stem, just as she had gripped oars so many thousands of times in her life.

"That's the first time she's done that since her stroke," said Tina, her smile reflecting both pride and enthusiasm as she reinforced her point. "No one told her how. She did it herself, on her own terms."

That little gesture of reaching for the wine glass makes it obvious that Ernie is not quitting on herself any more than she ever quit on rowers. Her determination is evident even though she spends a good part of her days dozing and, when awake, being uncharacteristically quiet…and serene.

The wineglass moment epitomizes what her life has been about. Now in her nineties and frail, she continues to reach out, fiercely determined to pursue goals that most people would think impossible.

At age ninety-seven, her goal was to hold a wine glass. At age twenty-nine, her goal was to create a rowing club for women. With that decision, Ernie had taken her first courageous steps from wannabe to doer, traveling into uncharted territory as she reached for the unknown.

She had separated herself from the pack and had taken tremendous risks in a venture that could have failed. Her journey, an intrusion on a male-dominated hostile culture, forced her to use whatever creative powers she had to transcend an environment where hidebound rules dictated what women could do.

In doing so she became the "mother" of women's rowing in the United States, and in the process she transformed her husband from a man of the establishment to a supporter of women's rowing. Ernest quietly and bravely proved that, despite his culture, he had the stature to help make rowing for women happen. He would have it no other way because of his deep love for his wife and daughter.

Hindsight brings 20/20 vision. We now see clearly that Ernie's persistence manifested itself as a blessing for organized competitive and recreational rowing in the United States, where women now constitute as strong a presence as men. Ernie's genius proved that both sexes could share equally in the joys and responsibilities of sending shells through water, experiencing the mysterious essence that is so fundamental to rowing.

Bibliography and Sources

Aside from numerous interviews, I have drawn on many of my own rowing experiences and my own conclusions from those experiences in writing this biography. However, nine books were enormously helpful in providing background.

Baltzell, E. Digby (1979). *Puritan Boston and Quaker Philadelphia.* Boston: Beacon Press.

Boyne, Daniel J. (2000). *The Red Rose Crew: A True Story of Women, Winning, and the Water.* New York: Hyperion.

Churbuck, D.C. (1988). *The Book of Rowing.* Woodstock, NY: Overlook Press.

Halberstam, David (1985). *The Amateurs.* New York: Fawcett Books.

Lewis, Linda (1992). *Water's Edge: Women Who Push the Limits in Rowing, Kayaking & Canoeing.* Emeryville, CA: Seal Press.

Martin, Arthur E. (1990). *Life in the Slow Lane.* Portsmouth, NH: Peter E. Randall Publisher.

Rivinus, Marion W. *Life Along the Schuylkill.* Privately published.

Stowe, William A. (2005). *All Together: The Formidable Journey to the Gold with the 1964 Olympic Crew.* New York, Lincoln, Shanghai: iUniverse Inc.

Sweeney, Joe. *The History of the Penn Athletic Club Rowing Association.* Published on the Internet at http://www.boathouserow.org/pac/pachist1.html

I have also drawn on my previous research for an article I wrote on rowing for Vol. II of the Encyclopedia of *World Sports, Vol. II,* published by ABC-CLIO Inc., Santa Barbara, CA, 1996; and my own work in preparing a thirtieth anniversary slide-tape show on the history of the Alden Ocean Shell Association. Subsequently I made the work available to the Mystic Seaport Museum.

In addition, I found much useful information in a collection of uncatalogued material the Bayer family donated to the National Rowing Foundation with a head office in Stonington, CT. The NRF has turned over the materials to the G.W. Blunt White Library at the Mystic Seaport Museum in Mystic, CT as source material for an eventual exhibit on rowing history. The Bayer family also lent me two other large boxes of uncatalogued material such as news clippings, photos, and programs from which I have been able to draw information and images.

ABOUT THE AUTHOR

LEW CUYLER AND HIS WIFE, HARRIET, LIVE IN PITTSFIELD, Massachusetts, and they both row on Lake Onota, about a mile away from their home. Educated at South Kent School in Connecticut, where he learned to row, and at Amherst College in Massachusetts, where he was coxswain, rower. and assistant coach for the rowing club, he spent most of his career as a journalist in western Massachusetts. At various times he was reporter, editor, and sometime photographer for three newspapers. He also worked for several years as a freelance writer, photographer, and producer of slide/ tape shows.

In 1995, he retired from his job as business editor for *The Berkshire Eagle* in Pittsfield to found a rowing club, now known as BRASS, the Berkshire Rowing and Sculling Society, and to establish a rowing business, Berkshire Sculling Inc., which leases and sells single rowing shells.

Along with his wife, he competes regularly in masters rowing regattas, both in the United States and abroad. For several years he coached rowing at the BRASS boathouse on Lake Onota, and before then from a trailer that he drove each day to the Stockbridge Bowl in Stockbridge, Massachusetts. For three seasons he was a guest coach at the Florida Rowing Center.

He and his first wife, who is deceased, have two children who live in Oregon and are now in their forties.

He serves on the board of the Alden Ocean Shell Association and for the past several years has been editor of its quarterly newsletter, *The Catch*. He is also a member of US Rowing, the Masters Rowing Association, and the Lake Onota Preservation Association.

Lew has rowed all shells but he is primarily a single sculler.

"Rowing puts it all together, physically and spiritually," he says. "Sending a shell through early morning quiet water provides an exhilarating fusion of body, mind, water, and air. There's nothing quite like the wholeness of the experience. Once you begin to get it, you never want to stop. It's addictive. ...A passion."

During the cold weather months, Lew skis, using three disciplines: alpine, telemark, and cross-country.

John B. Kelly Sr., Olympic oarsman from Philadelphia who won three golds in two Olympiads, presides over Schuylkill River in Philadelphia, commemorated by statue near finish line. He and his son, John B. Jr., a four-time Olympian, were major forces in shaping the city's rowing culture   *Lew Cuyler*

A NOTE ON PHOTOS:

During the research for this biography I found nearly 1,000 photos taken of Ernestine during her life and all of them were uncatalogued. A few years ago Tina and Ernestine Bayer gave boxes of papers and photos to the National Rowing Foundation for possible use in a future rowing exhibit at the Mystic Seaport Museum. Additionally they made available two large boxes of similar materials to me for my research.

Most photos had no identification as to the photographer with the exception of the late Charles Came of York, ME whose wife granted permission to use his magnificent photo for the cover as well as one another in Chapter 21. I wish to thank both Hart Perry, executive director of the National Rowing Foundation, and Tina Bayer for allowing use of photos for this biography. I also want to thank the legions of unidentified photographers whose work appears in this book. It was impossible to obtain their names.